Lecture Notes in Computer Science

Lecture Notes in Artificial Intelligence 15583

Founding Editor

Jörg Siekmann

Series Editors

Randy Goebel, *University of Alberta, Edmonton, Canada*
Wolfgang Wahlster, *DFKI, Berlin, Germany*
Zhi-Hua Zhou, *Nanjing University, Nanjing, China*

The series Lecture Notes in Artificial Intelligence (LNAI) was established in 1988 as a topical subseries of LNCS devoted to artificial intelligence.

The series publishes state-of-the-art research results at a high level. As with the LNCS mother series, the mission of the series is to serve the international R & D community by providing an invaluable service, mainly focused on the publication of conference and workshop proceedings and postproceedings.

Jason Thompson · Ivana Stankov
Editors

Multi-Agent-Based Simulation XXV

25th International Workshop, MABS 2024
Auckland, New Zealand, May 6, 2024
Revised Selected Papers

 Springer

Editors
Jason Thompson 🄳
The University of Melbourne
Parkville, VIC, Australia

Ivana Stankov 🄳
University of South Australia
Adelaide, SA, Australia

ISSN 0302-9743   ISSN 1611-3349 (electronic)
Lecture Notes in Computer Science
Lecture Notes in Artificial Intelligence
ISBN 978-3-031-88016-2   ISBN 978-3-031-88017-9 (eBook)
https://doi.org/10.1007/978-3-031-88017-9

LNCS Sublibrary: SL7 – Artificial Intelligence

This Springer imprint is published by the registered company Springer Nature Switzerland AG
The registered company address is: Gewerbestrasse 11, 6330 Cham, Switzerland

If disposing of this product, please recycle the paper.

Preface

Multi-Agent-Based Simulation (MABS) is a powerful tool used to inform policy decisions across a variety of applied domains. The collaboration of researchers from Multi-Agent Systems (MAS) engineering, simulation, and the social, economic, and organizational sciences is widely recognized for fostering cross-disciplinary innovation. This synergy has been a significant source of inspiration for the development of knowledge in the field. The MABS workshop series is dedicated to facilitating collaboration between researchers interested in MAS engineering and simulation and those focused on understanding and developing effective solutions to model complex social, socio-ecological, and socio-technical systems in areas such as economics, management, and the broader social sciences. In all these disciplines, agent-based theories, metaphors, models, analyses, experimental designs, empirical studies, and methodological principles converge on simulation to achieve explanations and predictions, explore and test hypotheses, and ultimately refine designs and systems.

This book constitutes the refereed post-conference proceedings of the 25th International Workshop on Multi-Agent-Based Simulation, MABS 2024, which took place in Auckland, New Zealand, from May 6, 2024, in conjunction with the 23nd International Conference on Autonomous Agents and Multi-Agent Systems (AAMAS 2024). This year's workshop focused on 'Modelling and Simulation of Societies' and encouraged submissions in areas including simulation methodology and tools, simulation of social and intelligent behavior, diverse applications, and simulation analytics. The 7 full papers included in this volume were carefully selected from 11 submissions through single-blinded review by at least 3 reviewers and single-blinded re-reviewed, incorporating insights from the discussions held during the workshop while retaining their original contributions.

The workshop could not have taken place without the contribution of numerous individuals. We extend our heartfelt gratitude to Pascal Perez for delivering an inspiring invited talk titled "From drug epidemics to urban futures. A life with agents!", as well as to all the participants, who engaged in a lively debate during the presentation of the papers. We are also grateful to all Program Committee members for their diligent efforts in reviewing the papers.

February 2025

Jason Thompson
Ivana Stankov

Organization

General and Program Chairs

Jason Thompson   University of Melbourne, Australia
Ivana Stankov   University of South Australia, Australia

Steering Committee

Frédéric Amblard   Toulouse 1 Capitole University, France
Luis Antunes   University of Lisbon, Portugal
Paul Davidsson   Malmö University, Sweden
Emma Norling   University of Sheffield, UK
Mario Paolucci   National Research Council, Italy
Jaime S. Sichman   University of São Paulo, Brazil
Samarth Swarup   University of Virginia, USA
Takao Terano   Tokyo Institute of Technology, Japan
Harko Verhagen   Stockholm University, Sweden

Program Committee

Jason Thompson   University of Melbourne, Australia
Harko Verhagen   Stockholm University, Sweden
Nicolas Verstaevel   Université Toulouse 1 Capitole, France
Fjalar de Haan   University of Melbourne, Australia
Nathalie Van Der Wal   Delft University of Technology, The Netherlands
Fabian Lorig   Malmö University, Sweden
Loïs Vanhée   Umeå University, Sweden
Shah Jamal Alam   Habib University, Pakistan
Liu Yang   Southeast University, China
Bill Kennedy   George Mason University, USA
Nick Gotts   .
Ruth Meyer   Ernst Mach Institute, Germany
Ivana Stankov   University of South Australia, Australia
Samarth Swarup   University of Virginia, USA
Gustavo Giménez-Lugo   Federal University of Technology-Paraná, Brazil
Jean-Pierre Muller   CIRAD, France

Contents

MABS Methodology and Tools

Creating a Serious Game on Top of an Agent-Based Simulation, an Applied Case to Crisis Management and Population Evacuation

Mathieu Bourgais[1]([✉]), Arnaud Saval[2], Pierrick Tranouez[2], Olivier Gillet[3], and Eric Daudé[3]

[1] INSA Rouen Normandie, Normandie Univ, LITIS UR 4108, 76000 Rouen, France
`mathieu.bourgais@insa-rouen.fr`
[2] Université Rouen Normandie, EA LITIS, Mont-Saint-Aignan, France
[3] CNRS, Normandie Université, UMR 6266 IDEES, Mont-Saint-Aignan, France

Abstract. Serious games have become widely prevalent, manifesting either as board games or role-playing experiences, designed to train individuals to think and respond in intricate scenarios that are often challenging to replicate and control in real life. Concurrently, numerous agent-based simulations, wherein simulated actors exhibit complex behaviors, are being developed to delve into the potential dynamics of intricate systems.

This paper introduces a fusion of these two methodologies, where a serious game built upon an agent-based simulation immerses users in conditions as closely resembling crisis management scenarios as possible. This amalgamation is not without its challenges, as serious games come with specific requirements that may clash with existing simulation frameworks. These include real-time interaction with the simulation, precise replay of given scenarios, an engaging display to captivate players, and the ability to manage multiple users playing different roles simultaneously on the same simulation.

To do so, the ESCAPE-SG serious game is presented. It is crafted on the foundation of ESCAPE, an established agent-based model aimed at simulating mass evacuations of populations from areas facing significant natural or technological hazards. The encountered challenges and the solutions devised to overcome them are outlined. Additionally, a software architecture is proposed to facilitate the connection between an agent-based simulation and a front-end display, serving as an interface for users.

Keywords: Agent-based simulation · Serious Games · Evacuation

1 Introduction

Institutional actors in charge of inhabited areas may face dangerous phenomena, whether of natural origin (floods, tsunamis, volcanic eruption) or technological (toxic cloud emitted by industrial plant). Decision making during these events

J. Thompson and I. Stankov (Eds.): MABS 2024, LNAI 15583, pp. 3–14, 2025.
https://doi.org/10.1007/978-3-031-88017-9_1

is crucial to protect exposed people inside these areas. One way to get ready for these extreme events is to train in advance, what is currently carried out through life-size training courses for the whole crisis management unit [22]. These training sessions often take the appearance of serious games [14] where a predefined scenario is played steps by steps with a careful analysis of results compared to an optimal solution at each step.

The primary goal of serious games, contrary to classical games where the objective is to entertain users, is to teach new knowledge to players through their participation and interaction with the game environment. [9]. This means that even if a serious game looks like a classical game, for example using pen and paper, a set of card or other kinds of pawns, the way it works answers other standards. Most of the serious games take the form of a social simulation or a role-playing game [27]. The game is run by a game master who helps the players make decisions in a believable environment. Then, the consequences of these decisions, which may put the game in a new state, are presented by the game master. At the end of the game, the game master shows and comments the results so that players understand what happened during the scenario they discovered. To increase the reality of the game and the panel of available scenarios, the simulation of the environment may be done through a computer simulation. The main point is that none of the decisions made by players should lead to situations not controlled by the game master or designers; each action must make sense in terms of the training and coaching objectives, and the results of these actions, whether good or bad in terms of the game's objectives, must be, if not known, at least within the range of solutions accepted by the game designers.

Indeed agent-based simulations are a meaningful framework for the study of a large variety of situations where humans interact in a very detailed environment [16]. Just concerning the use case of evacuation, there exists simulations of building evacuation [32], of cities evacuation [11] up to evacuations of regions [2], with various level of decision making complexity for the agents [6]. All these simulations, with their many parameters and random processes, produce a vast amount of data that researchers analyze to establish evolutionary scenarios based on probabilities of occurrence.

ESCAPE is such an agent-based evacuation-oriented simulation framework [11]. It is aimed at researchers whose works focus on the analysis of territorial vulnerabilities and mass population evacuation strategies. It provides intuitive tools for building spatial and social data, as well as libraries in the GAMA modeling platform [29] for fine-tuned modeling of mobility behaviors. Coupled with Open-Mole software [24], the ESCAPE suite can be used to explore numerous research hypotheses in "what-if" and "how-to" mode, such as a volcanic eruption [17]. ESCAPE requires the calibration of numerous parameters and exploration of a large number of scenarios to produce territorial diagnosis and implementation of crisis management plan. In this sense, ESCAPE is less a training tool than a support tool to evaluate different strategies, which is a challenge while switching it to a serious-game in respect to the mentionned constraints. ESCAPE-SG [13] is therefore a serious game built on top of ESCAPE, but conceived and designed as a training tool for crisis management. To do so, multiple players have to be able to interact with the running simulation, with various roles and different actions to perform. At the same time, a game manager should be able to run a scenario with external events. Finally, the game should be able to display the useful information in real time as well as ending statistics to measure the performance of the taken decisions and actions. These conditions are not met with the existing frameworks where detailed agent-based simulation of evacuation are implemented.

Section 2 of this articles discusses the previous works done with agent based simulations and serious games, in particular in the context of mass evacuation. Section 3 presents the challenges which come with building a serious game on top of an existing agent based simulation of an evacuation while Sect. 4 details the discussion about the implementation of such method on a specific use case. Finally, Sect. 5 concludes the article.

2   Related Works

Agent based simulations have been widely used to study complex systems involving human decisions and behaviors. They enable to recreate complex situations, for example social or environmental, and test various conditions of evolution of such complex systems. This section focuses on the reviews of agent based simulations and serious games about disaster risk management and population evacuation.

2.1   Simulating Evacuation

Evacuation of population under hazardous conditions is a case of social simulations [16] with an importance given to the spatial dimension [12]: an evacuation starts with a situation under normal conditions when something happens (it may be an alert sign or an sudden event) and people switch their normal behavior to abnormal conditions. Many works simulate the evacuation from the inside of a building with hundreds of agents [6,32]. Indeed a close environment with a fewer number of agents enables to implement a more complex behavior, with cognitive, affective and social dimensions as well as a fine description of architecture and geometries.

There are also city-scale simulations of evacuation. Taillandier *et al.* [29] simulate the evacuation of an urban area under flood. Each agent represents a pedestrian trying to find a shelter from a flood, following advises communicated by institutions. The same type of work may be done on a bigger geographical area with a bushfire as the hazard to evacuate from [2]. Finally, Daude *et al.* [11] proposes ESCAPE, a tool to model and simulate massive population evacuations in territories which can be described by very descriptive land-use data and network transportation system. In ESCAPE, agents which represent individual human may use different types of transport systems, starting as a pedestrian and then driving a car for example, to achieve their goals. ESCAPE offers a powerful Driving-skill pursuit model [26] and the agents have evolving knowledge of their travel environment. They can thus have knowledge of "experienced" traffic conditions, for example by memorizing the time spent by each person in traffic jams, as well as more macroscopic traffic conditions, which allows some agents to benefit from optimized routes. This framework has been used to simulate massive evacuation in the case of volcanic eruption [17] and of flooding [19].

2.2 Serious Games and Hazardous Situations

Serious games are playful activities which have, by learning, a serious goal on top of entertaining [9]. Learning is based on interactions with the model that simulates the crisis domain and on interactions between participants to collaborate and succeed in solving a certain number of tasks. Marne [21] proposes five common denominators for this type of game. The *challenges* are the problems given to the player; *Significant actions* correspond to the steps taken by the player to resolve these challenges; the *game engine* is the simulator which reacts to the player's actions; the *graphical interface* linked to the engine and the player which makes it possible to give a playful aspect to both the problems and the simulator; finally, a *script* that allows the levels of difficulty offered to evolve according to the desired educational progression.

Serious games have been applied in the field of disaster risk management where they may rise awareness about the consequences of catastrophes. In 2018, 45 serious games about disaster risk management were surveyed [27]. This includes a board game aiming at raising awareness about environmental disaster in the multicultural context of the Caribbean [10] or the "Don't Stop !" video game where users play the role of stakeholders who need to prevent damages before critical situation [15]. This latter video game has been expanded lately on the more specific topic of evacuations in front of a flood [18], proving the subject is still active in the community.

Some serious video games (that is to say serious games that uses video games technique as their core mechanics) rely on agent based simulations and multi-agent systems. Adam *et al.* propose a serious game about urban planning in the context of sustainable transport in cities [1]. In this game, users play the role of a group of people responsible for decisions on the urban landscape and the reaction of the population living in the city is generated through a multi-agent system. This technical design may be found in other works but specifically in the context of risk management and emergency evacuation as with the SPRITE game [28] or LitoSim [4]. The goal is to take actions that will have impact on the future catastrophe, the simulation is not in real time as the game simulate multiple months. With the same principle in mind, Moatty *et al.* developed a serious game about the evacuation of a population during a flood using an existing complex model of evacuation created with a multi agent system [29].

2.3   Synthesis

This section reviewed multiple agent-based simulations of large urban areas and evacuation of their population, and then discussed some existing serious games about disaster risk management. However, only few works combine these two field. From the simulation point of view, integrating game mechanisms would help popularize the results to a broader audience. From the serious game point of view, integrating an agent based simulation would make the result closer to a video game which is now a powerful language to communicate complex ideas to people [5].

One of the problem about using an agent based simulation into a serious "video" game in order to study the evacuation of populations on large urban area comes from the technologies used. Even if there exist multiple platforms to perform this type of simulation [3, 20, 30, 33], each with its own strengths and weaknesses, these tools are not suitable to integrate a complex interface which enables users to input discrete event into the simulation which operates in a continuous time.

3   From Simulations to Serious Games: Challenges

This section discusses the process used to create a serious game [26] about disaster risk management by taking its foundations in an existing evacuation simulation tool [13]. More specificaly, the objective is to create a multiplayer game, where each player has a specific role and may take actions while the simulation is running.

3.1   Simulating Evacuation at a City Level

The ESCAPE project [11] allows to simulate the evacuation of wide territories confronted to catastrophic events with citizens and civil servants (policemen, firefighters) represented by agents in the system. It's possible to first simulate the dynamics of the territory, such as the flow of vehicles under normal conditions, before injecting an event (e.g. an evacuation order or a volcanic eruption) that is perceived by agents, who will then react by modifying their behavior [8]. More precisely, the ESCAPE project is composed by the following elements:

- **Environment**: the land-use (buildings, forest, river) and road networks of the studied area are modeled. The pedestrian area are included as well as the type of the buildings (school, hospital, residential, etc.). A tool using R-Shiny has been developed to directly produce environment data gathered from OpenStreetMap [23]. All these data are pre-processed before being included in the simulation. Building the environment with open data enables to quickly adapt the project to a new use case about a new area.
- **Agents**: each person is represented by its own agent, and households can be represented as a set of agents. In order to create an agent population at a size coherent with demographic statistics, a sample of real people is

reproduced from census data. Generative synthetic population libraries [7] are then applied to this sample in order to generate a population of the correct size, with agents having characteristics as close as possible to the real studied population. There are also vehicles agents which may be used by people, i.e. cars, trucks, buses, bicycles and motorcycles. The flow dynamics on ordinary days is reproduced using both household travel survey and traffic data measured on the network.

- **Hazard**: hazards and theirs dynamics can be modeled directly or have their geographical footprint uploaded from geographical information system as time-step layers defining their spatial and temporal dynamics. Interactions between agents and hazards dynamics can be modeled to reproduce casualties, or any impact on the environment (e.g. speed reduction) depending on the catastrophe implemented.

ESCAPE is then useful to simulate territorial dynamics, both:

- **Under normal circumstances** : each agent follows its own schedule for the day. This includes going to work, taking care of their children who go to school, going to grocery store or going back to their home among other activities. To perform these activities agents may choose among different mobility modalities depending on their starting and ending point. Once in a vehicle, the shortest path to the destination is followed. Agents may use different types of vehicles to go to their destination target (starting as pedestrian, taking a car, then a bus and maybe ending with a bicycle). The vehicle is chosen based on the household travel survey as well as depending on the lowest estimated time to move from one point to another.
- **Under crisis situation** : when perceiving a hazard (either by seeing it, by hearing an alarm or a message on the radio), agents may change their behavior and give up their normal schedule. Depending on their own characteristics and the received message, they may either choose between evacuating or confining. To do so, each agent may use multiple transportation mode depending on the configuration estimated as the fastest.

Operationalization of crisis management is modeled through different actions taken by authorities such as the trigger of different types of alarms (global such as cell broadcast and local such as siren or mobile alarms set). These alarms may be heard by people which in return will decide or not to follow instructions. This means that not all agents either evacuate or confine shortly after the notification, but may still pursue their activities. This decision making process is fixed by the modeler through the use of different parameters or probabilities functions provided by ESCAPE tools and calibrated upon population surveys [17].

3.2   From ESCAPE to ESCAPE-SG

The ESCAPE project has been extended into the ESCAPE-SG serious game [13, 26]. The main goal of this operation is to create a training tool which is more understandable than a simulation, but provides realistic dynamics and scenarios. The key features of the ESCAPE-SG serious game are then:

- The overall setting is the evacuation of an urban environment, from a part of a town to a few nearby towns. For this, players should be able to interact with the running simulation (ex. to close a road, checking an information such as the number of peoples in a shelter or to select antenas to switch-on alarm system).
- Several players, each with a dedicated role (i.e. mayor, civil servant, road manager), should be able to play together on the same simulation at the same time. They may act on a medium or large scale: evacuate such or such building or area, block a road, intervene on a fire, etc. but the evacuating individuals are ran by the simulation. Likewise, a game manager should be able to trigger events during the game.
- The traffic situation inside the simulation should be displayed according to different temporalities: one in which simulated time is equivalent to real time, and also discrete (x3, x10) or continuous (from 1 to 10) accelerated modes that allows to stay within game durations consistent with the time allowed by players or game managers.
- Taking the fact that each role has its own actions available, players need to have feedback from the game to understand the consequences of their actions.

To integrate all these features, ESCAPE-SG has been implemented by using the SUMO platform [20] for the traffic simulation, and a custom multi-agent system in JAVA which runs the detailed individual interactions between mobile agents, beyond what is possible in SUMO. This MAS acts as an intermediate between SUMO and the Unity game engine [31] which is used for the ESCAPE-SG 3D graphics front-end. Indeed, the ESCAPE simulation is running on the GAMA platform which does not enables to easily act in multiplayer upon a simulation running in continuous time. If GAMA graphical interface allows to display simulation information, it is not meant to manage intensive graphical input from several players at once. It is also not able of synthesizing input from several different graphical interfaces computed on distant networked computers. Finally, GAMA cannot either be interrupted and resumed, or have internal values modified by external programs. It was as a consequence not the right software tool for the back-end.

Figure 1 shows the screen of the game manager watching a particular spot on the road network with ESCAPE-SG. Buildings and vehicles are displayed in three dimensions and the interface shows the various actions which may be taken. Each user watches a similar screen but may focus on an other place of the simulated area. They may access only their available actions. Figure 2 shows a more macroscopic view of the simulated territory, in which traffic conditions can be distinguished, synthesized here by color gradients on the sections.

Fig. 1. View of the manager role in the ESCAPE-SG serious game

Fig. 2. Overview of the simulated area in the city of Rouen

4   Generalizing the Process

Section 3 presented a use case where a serious game is built upon an existing agent based simulation of a city evacuation. This section discusses in a broader way the challenges related to the development of a serious game starting from an existing agent based simulation of an evacuation situation. The goal of this section is to present a general software architecture to ease the development of future serious video games.

4.1   Creating a Serious Game from a Simulation

As mentioned previously, one of the main challenge deals with the fact that players have to perform their actions while the simulation is running; in other words, this means triggering discrete events over a continuous simulation.

Figure 3 shows the software architecture developed to ensure that players could act over a running agent-based simulation. The system may be decomposed in three parts : the back-end where the simulation runs, the front-end which serves as an interface with players and an API which makes the connection between back-end and front-end.

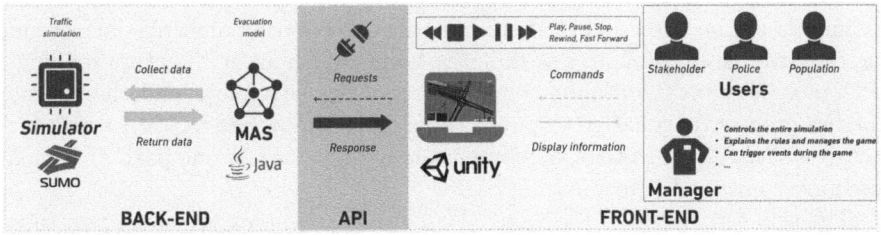

Fig. 3. Global software architecture for the creation of a serious game on top of an agent-based simulation

For ESCAPE-SG, instead of keeping one integrated solution for the back-end as it is the case in ESCAPE, the crisis simulation is performed by two systems communicating together as can be seen on Fig. 3. The multi-agent system (MAS) models people perception, decision-making and a part of their interactions. The simulator computes the next position of all mobile agents, depending on their current objective, mobility, and interactions with the hazard and other agents. The simulator computes the new location of each agent and sends it to the MAS which forwards it to the REST API for display.

On the front-end side, each user has its own client displaying a graphical interface. Depending on the role of each player, the actions available upon the simulation are different. Each action performed at any time by any player is sent to a REST API as a command. This command is then passed on to the MAS which modifies the environment settings. The set of commands includes closing a road or changing the direction of traffic, opening shelters or triggering alarms for example.

Lastly, the game manager has a dedicated interface. With a dedicated set of actions, the game manager may run a given scenario acting on the environment or the hazardous condition by sending commands to the API. This way, the game manager is seen as a player with a specific role.

4.2   General Discussion

To ensure an efficient serious game, in regard to the notions learnt by participants, it is important to put the player as close as possible to the real case situation [27] while having a multiplayer experience [25]. These two principles guided the creation of the software architecture described by Fig. 3.

Let's take an example of action: closing a road as the mayor during the evacuation. To mimic the real world, the player needs to implement this action by selecting the specific road to close and then close it few minutes after the order was given, simulating the time an employee would take to effectively close the road in real life. Multiple actions follow the same principle: either their effect is differed in time or their consequences will start to have an impact multiple minutes after they were decided.

The same problems arise on the game manager side: the hazard triggered have an effect over the simulation for multiple hours. Hence, the simulation flow of time should be altered in order to have a game covering multiple days around the catastrophe playable in few minutes/hours. With an architecture making a difference between the atomic computation of the next move and the decision making process, it is easier to pause the simulation or fast-forward it; as each part is waiting for the other, a command may be passed to one part which may disconnect until it is executed.

The goal for realism of the game also implies a complex graphical user interface. In the real life, stakeholders have a partial knowledge of the events. By implementing one client per role, each player as access to only partial information from the simulation and needs to communicate with the other players before making a decision. With the same principle, each role only has access to a sample set of all the possible actions, reflecting its real life capacities. All these reasons imply the use of a front-end which is not integrated with the back-end, a modularity that eases a personalized display.

5   Conclusion

This paper presents the challenges coming with the creation of a serious game about disaster risk management crafted on an existing agent-based simulator of mass evacuation. The creation of the serious game ESCAPE-SG [26] from the ESCAPE project [11] is described as an initial use case. This paper uses this particular case to extract a more general discussion on the challenges arising when building a serious game from an existing agent based simulation, especially in the field of disaster risk management.

In the future, the ESCAPE-SG serious game should be tested with crisis managers to assess its capacity to improve the existing training sessions. New scenarios on new areas will be implemented in ESCAPE-SG to demonstrate the generic nature of the project.

Acknowledgment. This work is supported by the ANR ESCAPE project, grant ANR-16-CE39-0011-01 (French Agence Nationale de la Recherche) and by the RIN Tremplin ESCAPE-SG project (Région Normandie).

References

1. Adam, C., Taillandier, F.: Un jeu sérieux pour sensibiliser aux enjeux d'une mobilité urbaine durable. Acad. J. Civil Eng. **40**(1), 29–32 (2022)
2. Adam, C., Taillandier, P., Dugdale, J., Gaudou, B.: BDI vs FSM agents in social simulations for raising awareness in disasters: a case study in Melbourne bushfires. Int. J. Inf. Syst. Crisis Response Manage. (IJISCRAM) **9**(1), 27–44 (2017)
3. Balmer, M., et al.: Matsim-t: architecture and simulation times. In: Multi-agent Systems for Traffic and Transportation Engineering (2009)
4. Beck, E., et al.: Chapter 9 - land use management for coastal flooding prevention: a participatory simulation platform applied to camargue (france). In: Pereira, P., Gomes, E., Rocha, J. (eds.) Mapping and Forecasting Land Use, pp. 193–221. Elsevier (2022). https://doi.org/10.1016/B978-0-323-90947-1.00002-8, https://www.sciencedirect.com/science/article/pii/B9780323909471000028
5. Bogost, I.: The rhetoric of video games. MacArthur Foundation Digital Media and Learning Initiative (2008)
6. Bourgais, M., Taillandier, P., Vercouter, L.: Ben: an architecture for the behavior of social agents. J. Artif. Soc. Soc. Simul. **23**(4) (2020)
7. Chapuis, K., Taillandier, P., Drogoul, A.: Generation of synthetic populations in social simulations: a review of methods and practices. J. Artif. Soc. Soc. Simul. **25**(2) (2022)
8. Chapuis, K., Taillandier, P., Gaudou, B., Drogoul, A., Daudé, E.: A multi-modal urban traffic agent-based framework to study individual response to catastrophic events. In: PRIMA 2018, pp. 440–448. Springer (2018)
9. Clark, C.A.: Serious Games. Viking, New York (1970)
10. Clerveaux, V., Spence, B., Katada, T.: Using game technique as a strategy in promoting disaster awareness in caribbean multicultural societies: the disaster awareness game. J. Disaster Res. **3**(5), 1–13 (2008)
11. Daudé, E., et al.: Escape: exploring by simulation cities awareness on population evacuation. In: ISCRAM 2019 (2019)
12. Daudé, E., et al.: Spatial risks and complex systems: methodological perspectives. Springer, From System Complexity to Emergent Properties (2009)
13. Daudé, É., Tranouez, P.: Escape–sg: un simulateur d'évacuation massive de population pour la formation des acteurs à la gestion de crise. Netcom. Réseaux, communication et territoires (34-3/4) (2020)
14. Di Loreto, I., Mora, S., Divitini, M.: Collaborative serious games for crisis management: an overview. In: 21st International Workshop on Enabling Technologies: Infrastructure for Collaborative Enterprises, pp. 352–357 (2012)
15. Gampell, A.V., Gaillard, J.C.: Stop disasters 2.0: video games as tools for disaster risk reduction. Int. J. Mass Emergencies Disasters **34**(2), 283–316 (2016)
16. Gilbert, N., Troitzsch, K.: Simulation for the Social Scientist. McGraw-Hill Education (UK) (2005)
17. Gillet, O., et al.: Modeling staged and simultaneous evacuation during a volcanic crisis of la soufrière of guadeloupe (france). SIMULATION p. 00375497231209998 (2023)
18. Hutama, I.A.W., Nakamura, H.: Expanding the conceptual application of "stop disasters!" game for flood disaster risk reduction in urban informal settlements. In: International Conference on Indonesian Architecture and Planning, pp. 581–599. Springer (2022)

19. Kevin, C., et al.: Exploring multi-modal evacuation strategies for a landlocked population using large-scale agent-based simulations. Int. J. Geogr. Inf. Sci. **36**(9), 1741–1783 (2022). https://doi.org/10.1080/13658816.2022.2069774

20. Krajzewicz, D., Erdmann, J., Behrisch, M., Bieker, L.: Recent development and applications of SUMO - Simulation of Urban Mobility. Int. J. Adv. Syst. Measurem. **5**(3&4), 128–138 (2012)

21. Marne, B., Wisdom, J., Huynh-Kim-Bang, B., Labat, J.M.: The six facets of serious game design: a methodology enhanced by our design pattern library. In: 21st Century Learning for 21st Century Skills: 7th European Conference of Technology Enhanced Learning, EC-TEL 2012, Saarbrücken, Germany, 18–21 September 2012. Proceedings 7, pp. 208–221. Springer (2012)

22. November, V., Créton-Cazanave, L.: La gestion de crise à l'épreuve de l'exercice EU SEQUANA. La Documentation Française (2017). https://shs.hal.science/halshs-01484782

23. OpenStreetMap contributors: planet dump retrieved from https://planet.osm.org, https://www.openstreetmap.org (2023)

24. Reuillon, R., Leclaire, M., Rey-Coyrehourcq, S.: Openmole, a workflow engine specifically tailored for the distributed exploration of simulation models. Futur. Gener. Comput. Syst. **29**(8), 1981–1990 (2013)

25. Roncoli, C.: Ethnographic and participatory approaches to research on farmers' responses to climate predictions. Climate Res. **33**(1), 81–99 (2006)

26. Saval, A., Bourgais, M., Daudé, É., Tranouez, P.: Escape-sg-un jeu sérieux pour mieux préparer les évacuations de masse. In: 31èmes Journées Francophones sur les Systèmes Multi-Agents, pp. 128–131 (2023)

27. Solinska-Nowak, A., et al.: An overview of serious games for disaster risk management-prospects and limitations for informing actions to arrest increasing risk. Int. J. Disaster Risk Red. **31**, 1013–1029 (2018)

28. Taillandier, F., Adam, C.: Games ready to use: a serious game for teaching natural risk management. Simul. Gaming **49**(4), 441–470 (2018)

29. Taillandier, F., Di Maiolo, P., Taillandier, P., Jacquenod, C., Rauscher-Lauranceau, L., Mehdizadeh, R.: An agent-based model to simulate inhabitants' behavior during a flood event. Int. J. Disaster Risk Red. **64**, 102503 (2021)

30. Taillandier, P., et al.: Building, composing and experimenting complex spatial models with the gama platform. GeoInformatica **23**, 299–322 (2019)

31. Unity: Game Engine. http://www.unity3d.com (2024)

32. Valette, M., Gaudou, B., Longin, D., Taillandier, P.: Modeling a real-case situation of egress using bdi agents with emotions and social skills. In: PRIMA 2018: Principles and Practice of Multi-Agent Systems: 21st International Conference, Tokyo, Japan, October 29-November 2, 2018, Proceedings 21, pp. 3–18. Springer (2018)

33. Wilensky, U., Evanston, I.: Netlogo: Center for Connected Learning and Computer-Based Modeling. Northwestern Univ, Evanston, IL (1999)

GENSIMO - A Generic Framework for Modelling Social Insurance Systems

Fjalar J. de Haan[1,2,3(✉)]⍟ and Jason Thompson[2,3]⍟

[1] School of Computing and Information Systems, Faculty of Engineering and Information Technology, The University of Melbourne, Parkville, Australia
[2] Melbourne Centre for Data Science, The University of Melbourne, Parkville, Australia
[3] Department of Psychiatry, Faculty of Medicine, Dentistry and Health Sciences, The University of Melbourne, Parkville, Australia
{fjalar.dehaan,jason.thompson}@unimelb.edu.au

Abstract. We report on the design, development and prototype testing of GENSIMO (GENeric Social Insurance MOdeling), a free and open-source software framework for modelling and simulation of social insurance systems. We discuss the conceptual and software design considerations of the framework in general before demonstrating how it works in detail by setting it up to model a particular social insurance scheme. We then present how we used this prototype set up to model the impact of a policy intervention on the workload of the insurer. While GENSIMO is under active development and we are a while away from serious verification and validation, this prototype testing shows realistic results.

Keywords: Social insurance · Julia · Agent-Based Modelling · Free and Open Source Software

1 Introduction

We report on the design, development and prototype testing of GENSIMO (GENeric Social Insurance MOdeling), a free and open-source software framework for modelling and simulation of social insurance systems. Typical examples of social insurance are workers' accident compensation schemes and social security services that provide unemployment benefits. We have a particular interest in road accident compensation schemes in Australia as this is our funding context (see the acknowledgements in Sect. 4). GENSIMO leverages the similarities amongst many schemes to provide a generic software framework that can be set up for, in principle, any scheme thus also enabling comparison. The software, under active development, is available as a Julia package under a GPLv3+ licence (https://github.com/gensimo/Gensimo) the current prototype is an application to the scheme of the Transport Accident Commission in Victoria, Australia (https://www.tac.vic.gov.au/).

We believe that modelling social insurance systems is societally important. Billions of public dollars are moved each year in schemes that touch millions of

© The Author(s), under exclusive license to Springer Nature Switzerland AG 2025
J. Thompson and I. Stankov (Eds.): MABS 2024, LNAI 15583, pp. 15–27, 2025.
https://doi.org/10.1007/978-3-031-88017-9_2

lives. Clearly, insurance organisations have not hitherto been going unmodelled. Insurers typically have high-quality statistical and actuarial expertise, either in-house or outsourced. What we aim to provide with GENSIMO is a complementary approach that not only aids in forecasting workloads and liabilities but, in doing so, provides a representation of the internal mechanics of insurance schemes. Our framework employs agent-based modelling (ABM) which allows us to directly model virtual clients interacting with a modelled scheme. Such a representation, we suggest, is an intuitive tool for policy experiments and scheme design.

Simulation models, and in particular ABMs, are not the mainstream approach in the social insurance context. Thus, we necessarily build from our own experience in this field and the broader ABM literature (which we assume the reader is familiar with). While GENSIMO's design and codebase are altogether new, we can draw on many years of experience developing models for social insurance systems. Of particular relevance are [3,4] which report on agent-based models for transport accidence insurance and workers compensation schemes, respectively. Most of our modelling work in this context is done in close collaboration with stakeholders which over the years has led to many lessons learnt, which were distilled in the form of guidelines for policy makers in [5].

A common feature in many social insurance schemes is that they are claim-based. Clients coming 'on scheme' have a claim with the insurer which typically affords them financial compensation for health care and injury rehabilitation services they receive. For example, in an road trauma context, a client comes on scheme after having been injured in a road crash. Depending on the scheme, services the insurer might recompense include items as surgery, physiotherapy, income compensation and adjustments to living arrangements. Taking this common feature as the basis, GENSIMO essentially follows virtual clients on their journey through the scheme. Clients have a bipartite representation, with one part modelling their overall health status, while the other part models their administrative status, i.e. their claim. Along their journey in the modelled system, clients encounter events such as undergoing assessments, requesting services and so on, each one of which may have consequences for their administrative and health states.

In the following, (Sect. 2) we present the design and development of the GENSIMO framework in general terms. After that, we report on its application to a particular insurance scheme as part of prototype testing (Sect. 3). We then compare two versions of a scheme to assess, amongst other things, impacts on workload. We end the paper with some brief conclusions (Sect. 4).

2   Design Overview of the GENSIMO Framework

2.1   Software Design Considerations

As research software, aiming to be a platform for innovation and geared towards use in actual policy settings, we think it obvious that GENSIMO be a download-able, free and open source software package. And so it is, as you can verify at https://github.com/gensimo/Gensimo where it is available under a GNU General Public Licence Version 3+. The GENSIMO package is under constant development. A version circa the original submission date—12 February 2024—of this paper to MABS2024 can be found at this GitHub commit: https://github.com/gensimo/Gensimo/commit/e2a0db7fca09d452f13d2f1d0f92e7041ac510fd.

We chose to develop GENSIMO using the Julia language [1] as it is fast and extremely suitable for technical computing. In addition to the many useful facilities the language offers 'out of the box', we make extensive use of several Julia packages. Amongst these, the most important are:

Agents.jl This is Julia's main package for agent-based modelling [2]. It is easy to use and proclaims to be fast, simple and providing extensive tools. You can find it at https://github.com/JuliaDynamics/Agents.jl.

POMDPs.jl This is Julia's key package for modelling Markov Decision Processes (MDPs). It can be found here http://juliapomdp.github.io/POMDPs.jl/latest/. The GENSIMO framework also provides facilities to model a social insurance system as an MDP. This provides a convenient representation of the empirical data and this makes it suitable for validation as well. This aspect of the framework is not discussed further in this paper.

Later in this paper we will discuss how GENSIMO is set up to model a particular social insurance scheme. In software terms, this means that we have set up a separate Julia package (not publicly available as it would disclose sensitive information) that uses the GENSIMO package. Now we will introduce GENSIMO as an agent-based modelling platform.

2.2   Agent-Based Modelling Aspects

The focal agents in GENSIMO models are of the `Client` type. The things that happen to these agents are the output variables of interest, whether considered individually or at the level of a 'cohort', i.e. a `Client`-agent population. The environment for `Client`-agents is the insurance scheme, the settings of which are provided through the so-called `Conductor` object (see Sect. 2.3). The `Conductor` object is used to initialise an Agents.jl object of type `AgentBasedModel` in which the `Client`-cohort lives. Below we discuss GENSIMO's agent types (Sect. 2.2.1), the structure of the `Client` agent type (Sect. 2.2.2) and the life cycle of `Clients` (Sect. 2.2.3).

2.2.1   Agent Types

In the stage of development at the time of initial submission of this paper, `Client` was the only agent type GENSIMO provided. Moreover, `Clients` did (and still do) not interact, so GENSIMO modelling at this stage is rather like micro-simulation. Various other GENSIMO agent types were already planned and several are now implemented, tested and usable. We summarise them in Table 1 as they play no role in the rest of this paper.

Table 1. Agent types in GENSIMO. Note that when this paper was initially submitted to MABS2024, only the Client type was available.

Type	Description	Fields
Client	Representation of a client of the social insurance scheme.	• Personalia (name, age etc.) • Health history (physical, mental etc.) • Claim log (service requests etc.)
Manager	Social insurance worker. Manages claims and approves or denies clients' service requests.	• Capacity (maximum concurrent #tasks)
Clientele	Service provision and task allocation environment.	• Client members • Managers (1 or more, each with task queue)
Provider	Allied-health (typically) provider. Certain service requests processed in interaction with these agents.	• Menu of services provided with ask price • Capacity (maximum concurrent #clients) • Servicing factor (over or under servicing) • Recovery factor (faster or slower than norm)

2.2.2 Client **Agent Structure**

The Client type, personalia aside, consists of two aspects (1) a history of states, and (2) an administrative event log which we identify as the client's claim. Consequently, a client object carries, at any point in the simulation, its entire history with it.

The history of states records the client's physical and mental health scores over time. In modelling terms, each state is a vector of floating point variables. How many variables one wants to consider and to which metrics they correspond would depend on the scheme and the availability of data. The history of states is thus a list of such vectors paired with the date at which that state is current.

The administrative event log is represented as an object of the Claim type. This object contains events, which are objects of type Event. Different sorts of events may happen to a client. Currently, we identify assessments, segmentation and service request events. An event has a date and an object detailing the change. For example, an assessment (a numerical score of a client's health state) event is simply a date with a score. A segmentation event also carries the tier and description of the service level the client is assigned to. A service request event carries a label describing the service requested, and the associated cost and workload.

Both the history of states and the claim objects are collections of date-state or date-change pairs. The framework provides a range of convenience functions to, for example, get a client's current state, segment, list of requests or the date of most recent change. Likewise there are convenience functions to add events. The user does not have to think about the internals of the Client object.

2.2.3 Client **Agent Life Cycle**

By 'life cycle' of a Client agent, we mean its journey through the simulated scheme. When a client comes 'on scheme', the scheme begins to deploy processes involving that client. As a consequence, the client's recovery is helped or hindered, while the insurer incurs costs, labour and liability. GENSIMO models this with a Client data type that keeps track of physical and mental health (as well as other factors) and various administrative events. The life cycle can thus be viewed a client state-changing machine.

The processes in the life cycle can be summarised in a quasi-sequential scheme as like in Fig. 1. While this life cycle is obviously incomplete in several ways, it is a realistic basis and it can be easily augmented. For example, routine processes like independent medical examinations or common law cases are not included but they easily can be—that is, insofar as they can be modelled at all. This also enables modularity, for example, a policy experiment might want to investigate different versions of the segmentation process—which is what we did in the prototype testing (see Sect. 3)—or alternative service decision deliberations.

Induction Client comes on scheme. Claim is opened.

Segmentation Client is allocated a service level based on health status or other personal parameters. A client may be re-segmented at later times.

Service request cycle Occurs zero or more times, depending on recovery trajectory.
  – *Service request* — A product or service the client is seeking compensation for.
  – *Service decision* — Process of deliberation culminating in the request being approved, denied or amended.
  – *Iatrogenic effects* — The impact the service decision process has on the health and satisfaction of the client. E.g. psychological ramifications of repeatedly denied requests.

Recovery Background overall improvement of client's condition over time (exponential). GENSIMO does not model medical aspects in detail.

Inactivation After a period of inactivity a client is deemed 'inactive' or exits the scheme, depending on the insurer.

Fig. 1. GENSIMO Flowchart of Client agent life cycle processes in quasi sequence.

2.3   Conductor: Keeping Time and Score

To run simulations, GENSIMO, provides the Conductor type. A Conductor object contains the (1) initial and final dates of the simulation timeline, (2) a Context object for settings, parameter values and probability distributions and, (3) the cohort of Client's. Specific implementations of GENSIMO then provide a simulate!(conductor::Conductor) function accepting a conductor to run the simulation on. As the simulation runs, the Client objects contained in the Conductor are updated in-place, growing their histories of state and claims. When simulate!() returns, the Conductor object can be used to extract results. GENSIMO provides a range of convenience functions to extract information, for individual clients as well as scheme-level aggregate statistics. Various plotting tools are available that accept a Conductor or Client object directly.

The framework uses a daily time step and dates are represented using the `Date` type from the Julia package `Dates`, that is, not as naked integers. The `simulate!()` function thus steps through every day from the initial to the final date set in the `Conductor` object. Every client, however, is on a personal clock, as it were. For each client, the timing, number and kind of events depend on the characteristics of that client only, most prominently the day of coming on scheme. The detailed modelling of what event is to occur when to a client clearly depends on the scheme under consideration. We will therefore discuss the details of the event timing, especially the service request cycle, as part of the setting up of GENSIMO for the scheme of the Transport Accident Commission in Victoria, Australia (Sect. 3.1).

3   Prototype - Setting up and Testing Gensimo

We have been emphasising the design principle that GENSIMO be a *generic* framework. To test the framework, however, one does need to implement a particular scheme. This could be a hypothetical, stylised scheme of course, and there would actually be virtue in doing it that way but we find ourselves in the fortunate situation that an actual social insurance organisation, the Transport Accident Commission (TAC) provides part of the funding for the model development. The TAC also provide their ample domain expertise and experience as well as their data. Importantly, they also have research questions they would like a modelling perspective on.

Thus, in addition to our ambition to provide with GENSIMO a generic framework, we are concurrently developing a 'digital twin' for the TAC based on it. Our interpretation of 'digital twin' is a computer model that is an intuitive representation of the TAC insurance scheme(s), that is, it needs to be recognisable and realistic to the TAC. Moreover, we want this model to be quantitatively realistic and accurate also—i.e. as 'close to the data' as possible. This means that we use the same state variables for our virtual clients' health states as the TAC uses internally, that they request the same (virtual) services as real clients at the same costs etc. To be clear, the model does *not* use individual client data. What we use are aggregates, averages, distributions etc.

3.1   Setting up GENSIMO as a TAC Digital Twin

To describe the setting up of GENSIMO as a TAC Digital Twin, we will follow the life cycle flow chart of Fig. 1. In passing, we will elaborate how the various data structures, like `Client`, are operationalised.

3.1.1   Induction

TAC clients have had a traffic accident. The accident date and health state at that moment are the first entry in the `Client` object's history of states. As mentioned, the health state of a GENSIMO `Client` is just a vector of 12 floating point variables, though it is easy to increase this number if required. Of these 12 variables, there are currently 3 that play a key role in the model:

- *Physical health* (φ) as a percentage of pre-accident health.
- *Mental health* (ψ) as a percentage of pre-accident health.
- *Satisfaction* with the scheme experience, as a percentage.

When creating a cohort of clients for a simulation, one could in principle populate these variables using the empirical probability distribution if data is available. For testing purposes we will be using uniformly random sampled clients. The model makes up a name, sex and age for a touch of realism, see Fig. 2.

Induction is very much a silent process in the model. Clients have an accident date and corresponding health status at the moment of instantiation of their Client objects. This essentially is all there is to it.

```
julia> client = Client()
Client ID: 5
 | Rebecca Matthews. 28 year-old female.
Status (2020-01-01):
 | φ = 0.7795488937126166
 | ψ = 0.2240473038573717
Claim (showing 0/0 newest events):
 | Empty claim.
```

Fig. 2. A random synthetic client, showing status (most recent health state) and claim events (none yet).

3.1.2 Segmentation

The segmentation process, as currently modelled, consists of two events. The first is an assessment of the clients needs, based on health status. The second is the actual assignment of the client to an organisational division, with the concomitant level of care.

Assessment

Assessing the clients needs determines their needs score, which is an integer between zero and 6, inclusive, with a higher number indicating greater needs. The model provides two ways of assigning a needs score to a client, (1) based on their mental and physical health states, and (2) randomly, based on the empirical distribution. The former may be more representative of actual practice, while the latter may reproduce actual data more readily. Needs scoring is done in the model right on the client's accident date.

Assignment

Segmentation means that a client is assigned an appropriate service level ('Tier'), which corresponds to an organisational sub-division. Depending on a client's segmentation, their case may be managed by as part of a single case manager's *portfolio* or as part of a *pool* of client assistance staff. Whether a client is managed in a pool or a portfolio has consequences for the decision times for service requests and thus for client satisfaction and workload associated with casemenagement of the client. Therefore, the segmentation strategy is a very important consideration in scheme design. As part of the prototype testing of the TAC Digital Twin, we have implemented two strategies:

BAU The current strategy. Needs scores zero to 3, inclusive are segmented to Tier 1 while scores 4 and above go to Tier 2. By and large, Tier 1 are managed in pools Tier 2 in portfolios.

NEW Here, an intermediate tier is added, yielding needs scores 0, 1 and 2 going to Tier 1, scores 3 and 4 to Tier 2 and everything above going to Tier 3. By and large only Tier 1 is managed in pools.

Thus we expect the number of clients managed in portfolios to increase. The modelling question is whether this leads to an overall increase in workload for the scheme, and if so, by how much.

It should be noted that this is a rather gross simplification of the actual segmentation process the TAC have. The actual process is not anything nearly so algorithmic and, moreover, we ignore entire parts of the client cohort here (notably clients with very severe injuries who are managed by a separate division altogether). In this paper, we are presenting a proof of concept of the modelling framework, not a faithful representation of TAC—the details that make the model a true digital twin are not disclosed.

3.1.3 Service Request Cycle

The bulk of a client's claim normally consists of service requests. When, how many and which services will be requested is here a key concern. As GENSIMO does not model a client's medical dynamics, the predicted claim evolution will be inaccurate at the individual level. Nonetheless, at the cohort level, clear patterns can be discerned in the data. Unsurprisingly, the closer to the accident, the more frequently a client can be expected to request a service. The intuitive explanation is simply that closer to the accident, the client *needs* those services as part of the recovery process. Ergo, the rate of service requests is inversely proportional to the health status of the client.

Empirically, we see clients' request volume declining roughly exponentially over time and consequently, we assume *typical* recovery to be exponential as well, gradually approaching pre-accident health status. (See below, under 'Recovery'). Combining this with the request rate being proportional to the client's health, we obtain an inhomogeneous Poisson-like process. The intensity of the process being (1) inversely proportional to the instantaneous health state and, because of the client's recovery trajectory, (2) exponentially declining over time.

Service request

—Every day, from the date the client comes on scheme, a sample is drawn from the Poisson-like process described above. This sample is the number of requests placed on that day. If the number is zero, which it often is, the service request cycle is aborted and neither the claim nor the history of state is updated (see below, under 'Recovery'). If the number is positive there are requests and these requests are drawn from the empirical distribution corresponding to the pool or portfolio environment the client is in. Thus, the kind of request (what service it is) as well as the cost and associated workload are in this sense random. Thus the client's claim will not make much medical sense. But at the cohort level the statistics ought to be realistic.

Service decision
—For each request, the scheme makes a service decision. The model makes the simplification that services are only ever accepted or denied. Moreover, this decision is logged immediately with the service request even though the associated workload may well exceed a single day. The workload is logged as part of the request so it still gets counted in the statistics as it should. The modelled version of the decision process is decidedly unsophisticated. Within the first 90 days after the accident, all requests are approved. After that, there is a flat rate of rejection of about 30%. While the 90 days blanket acceptance is not unrealistic, the flat rejection rate is and it should be considered a place holder, it is currently not informed by TAC data.

Iatrogenic effects
—The experience of clients with the scheme may have an impact on their recovery. At this point, we have included some hypotheses on these iatrogenic effects of the scheme. These are not validated with TAC data nor can we, at this point, adduce any e.g. psychological literature to substantiate. Again, they should be considered place holders. That said, we include a +1% physical health improvement for each approved request and a –1% psychological health deterioration as well as satisfaction for each denial.

3.1.4   Recovery

As discussed above, clients' recoveries are modelled as exponential trajectories. The recovery *rate* is inversely proportional to the age of the client at date of the accident. This of course means recovery will be slower the older the client is.

It should be noted that the history of states of a `Client` object is updated only on dates when service requests are also made. Any iatrogenic effects (see above) are then applied to this updated health state.

3.1.5   Inactivation

In principle, a claim is never closed. However, since clients recover exponentially to their pre-accident state—give or take iatrogenic effects—they will at some point cease to request new services. If a client has not requested anything for over 90 days, that client is considered 'inactive'. In reality, clients may of course come to request new services after a period of 'inactivity'. At the time of original submission, the model could not reproduce such cases. This functionality has been added since. Thus, the number of *active* clients is an important monitoring instrument and the model provides functions to extract it in various ways: at a certain time, as a time series and by tier.

3.2   Testing and Comparison of Two Segmentation Strategies

As an initial, proof-of-concept type, analysis we set the model up to investigate the consequences of a hypothetical new segmentation strategy (NEW) vis-à-vis an existing one (BAU). We discussed the differences between these segmentation strategies in Sect. 3.1. The main modelling question is how the changed strategy will affect the insurers workload—both workload overall and the expected shifts of load from one organisational division to another.

Segmentation strategy, in the model, is related to workload in the following way:

- Segmentation leads to clients being assigned to service level tiers, based on their health status.
- Service level tiers (2 for BAU and 3 for NEW) correspond to a client being managed as by a *pool* of client assistance staff or in a single case manager's *portfolio*.
- The time between a service being requested and the scheme's decision on it is different depending on whether the client is in a pool or a portfolio.
- This time to decision is a proxy for the workload associated with the service request.

There is, empirically, no obvious pattern relating pool versus portfolio to more or less workload, though there are differences at the level of services. This suggests that by and large the *overall* workload ought to not change dramatically. However, under the NEW strategy, a considerable class of clients that would have been assigned to a pool environment under the BAU strategy, are now assigned to portfolios. From data, we would expect the fraction of clients in portfolios to increase from about 24% to 44%. Thus we expect the workload to shift from pools to portfolios accordingly and the question is by how much.

3.2.1   Simulation Strategy

We ran batch simulations with cohorts of 1,000 clients. Clients have uniformly random initial health parameters and age between 0 and 100 years. In other words, we are not attempting yet to model an actual cohort—just a proof of concept with few assumptions on the client parameters. We simulate the period from 1 January 2019 to 1 January 2029, inclusive. Clients come on-scheme uniformly at random throughout that window, mimicking a constant flow of new clients into the scheme. Obviously, we are ignoring seasonal bursts, trends etc. We run 20 such simulations per scheme to obtain decent averages.

Summarising the main results, we find:

- Overall workload *decreases* by about 6%. A relatively small decrease (as anticipated) but not negligible—practically nor statistically—either.
- Workload in portfolios increases. With respect to the BAU the NEW strategy sees 74% more workload in porfolios.
- Workload in pools decreases. With respect to the BAU the NEW strategy sees 27% less workload in pools.
- The balance between workload in pool versus portfolio shifts from 80/20 to 62/37 going from BAU to NEW.

We note that an individual simulation of 1,000 clients over 10 years (i.e. roughly 3,560 time steps) takes approximately 20 s on a laptop (Lenovo X1

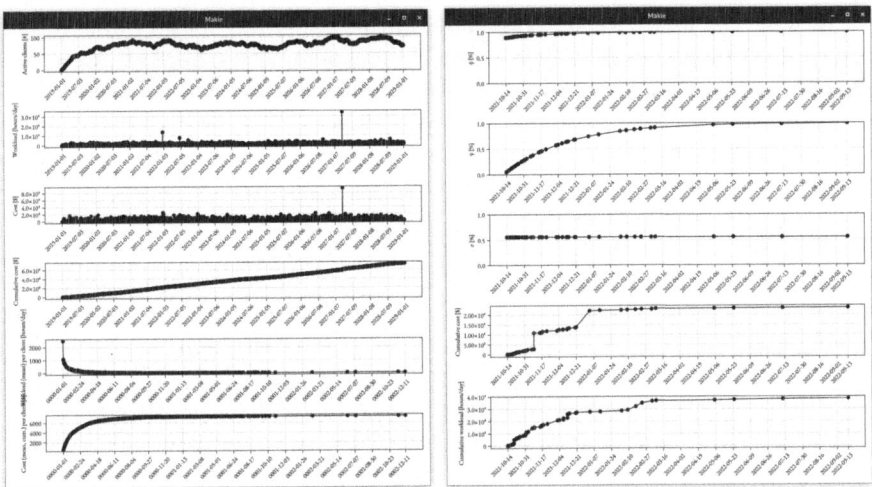

Fig. 3. Panel plots for simulations of a typical cohort (left) and a typical client (right).

Carbon running Fedora Linux 37 with a 12th Gen Intel Core i7-1255U @ 12x 4.7 GHz CPU and 16 GB RAM). In tests, we changed how clients entered the scheme over time from uniformly over the entire time frame to having them enter in a single burst in the first year. This changes the runtime to approximately 40 s. In the simulations for this paper, a single 20 simulation batch run thus takes in the order of 6–7 min.

4   Conclusions

This paper presented GENSIMO, a generic framework for modelling social insurance systems. We showed how it works by setting it up for a specific social insurance context, as a Digital Twin of the Transport Accident Commission (TAC) in Victoria, Australia. We then discussed early prototype testing which compared two segmentation strategies as to their impact on workloads for the insurer. Simulations are fast and at the current scale do not at all require any high-performance computing infrastructure. Initial results appear sensible though we do not claim this to constitute model verification.

When appraising the work presented, we should again stress that the framework, as well as the application as a digital twin, is under active development. Changes to the very structure of the generic framework are expected, as are many changes and improvements to the digital twin. Indeed, in the time between initial submission of this paper for MABS2024 in February and this revised version for the conference proceedings, many such changes and improvements have been made (see e.g. our discussion of the GENSIMO agent types in Sect. 2.2.1).

Likewise, the model version presented in this paper did not go through thorough verification and validation exercises. Model parameters, however, were typically chosen in realistic ranges as suggested by the distributions gleaned from the data. In some areas there is scope for decent statistical matching of the empirical data and model parameters. In particular, the stochastic process governing the timing and volume of service request could be so calibrated.

To the best of our knowledge, there is no other generic platform for social insurance modelling and simulation like GENSIMO. Indeed, there does not seem to be much modelling and simulation of social insurance systems around at all if we leave mainstream economic, statistical and actuarial approaches out of consideration. This, in spite of the obvious economic importance of these schemes (often amounting to considerable percentages of GDP) as well as the—in our view—academic appeal of the interdisciplinary challenge they present.

With GENSIMO then, we aim to provide a platform for research, policy innovation and collaboration. We hope that by making GENSIMO available as a free and open source software package, we can entice researchers to step into this arena and contribute to a public modelling knowledge base—whether by contributing to GENSIMO directly, by forking their own versions or developing entirely new frameworks. That is what we would like to contribute with GENSIMO.

Acknowledgements. The authors would like to gratefully acknowledge funding for this research from the NHMRC Centre of Research Excellence in Better Health Outcomes for Compensable Injury (NHMRC ID APP2007062, see also https://cre-rfrti.centre.uq.edu.au/) and the Transport Accident Commission (TAC, https://www.tac.vic.gov.au/). Special thanks to our liaisons at the TAC for their time, effort and input. Associate Professor Thompson is supported by Australian Research Council Future Fellowship FT220100650.

Disclosure of Interests. The authors have no other interests to disclose than those mentioned in the acknowledgements.

References

1. Bezanson, J., Edelman, A., Karpinski, S., Shah, V.B.: Julia: a fresh approach to numerical computing. SIAM Rev. **59**(1), 65–98 (2017). https://doi.org/10.1137/141000671, publisher: SIAM
2. Datseris, G., Vahdati, A.R., DuBois, T.C.: Agents.jl: a performant and featurefull agent-based modeling software of minimal code complexity. Simulation p. 00375497211068820, January 2022. https://doi.org/10.1177/00375497211068820, publisher: SAGE Publications Ltd STM
3. Thompson, J., Cruz-Gambardella, C.: Development of a computational policy model for comparing the effect of compensation scheme policies on recovery after workplace injury. J. Occupat. Rehabil. **32**(2), 241–251 (2022). https://doi.org/10.1007/s10926-022-10035-w

4. Thompson, J., McClure, R., de Silva, A.: A complex systems approach for understanding the effect of policy and management interventions on health system performance. In: Social-Behavioral Modeling for Complex Systems, pp. 809–831, April 2019. https://doi.org/10.1002/9781119485001.ch35
5. Thompson, J., et al.: A framework for considering the utility of models when facing tough decisions in public health: a guideline for policy-makers. Health Res. Policy Syst. **20**(1), 107 (2022). https://doi.org/10.1186/s12961-022-00902-6

Are Low Emission Zones Effective in Reducing Emissions and Ambient Air Pollution?

Hyesop Shin[1,5(✉)], Eric Silverman[1], Alison Heppenstall[1], Nick Malleson[2], Mario Ilic[3], Sonali Abeysinghe[3], and Tabea Sonnenschein[4]

[1] MRC/CSO Social and Public Health Sciences Unit, University of Glasgow, 90 Byres Road, Glasgow G12 8TB, UK
hyesop.shin@glasgow.ac.uk
[2] School of Geography, University of Leeds, Leeds LS2 9JT, UK
[3] Technical University of Munich, Arcisstraße 21, München, Germany
[4] Utrecht University, Amsterdam, The Netherlands
[5] School of Environment, University of Auckland, 1010 Auckland, New Zealand

Abstract. Glasgow, a major city in the UK, faces ongoing challenges with traffic congestion and high levels of air pollution. In response, Glasgow City Council introduced Scotland's first Low Emission Zone (LEZ) in June 2023. This study investigates the potential impacts of the LEZ on traffic flow, emissions and public health outcomes using an agent-based modelling approach. Using the SUMO traffic simulator, the work in-progress model simulates the complexity of urban traffic dynamics and the associated emissions. Preliminary results highlight emissions fluctuations influenced by traffic congestion and vehicle stops, with significant emissions reductions observed under LEZ-compliant scenarios. The study also identifies critical challenges, including traffic collisions due to inadequate infrastructure and limitations of real-time traffic data. These findings highlight the need for calibrated traffic patterns and infrastructure improvements to maximise the effectiveness of the current LEZ simulation.

Keywords: Low Emission Zone (LEZ) · Glasgow · Traffic Simulation · Emission · Air Quality · Simulation of Urban Mobility (SUMO)

1 Introduction

Air pollution in Glasgow has escalated into a critical public health issue. Despite increasing concerns, a significant gap exists in epidemiological research evaluating the impact of pollution on public health. This gap is particularly concerning given the rapid increase in vehicle numbers in Glasgow, leading to higher nitrogen oxides and particulate emissions [1,17]. In response, Glasgow has initiated Scotland's first Low Emission Zone (LEZ) on June 1, 2023. The LEZ aims to reduce air pollution and protect both pedestrians and drivers by targeting vehicles that do not meet up to date EURO standards.

J. Thompson and I. Stankov (Eds.): MABS 2024, LNAI 15583, pp. 28–36, 2025.
https://doi.org/10.1007/978-3-031-88017-9_3

However, the enforcement of the LEZ presents various challenges and uncertainties. Air pollution levels within the LEZ vary markedly across different roads, necessitating a thorough examination of these differences. In addition, the difficulty of providing real-time updates in air pollution modelling and the limited number of reliable monitoring stations further complicate the issue. Many previous studies on air pollution and health have relied on spatial interpolation and dispersion models, which tend to provide aggregated data on a monthly or yearly basis [2–4, 10, 11]. While this approach can illustrate the overall distribution of pollution effectively, it may not be particularly useful for policy intervention; such aggregated figures offer limited insights into the nuances of pollution levels, which are crucial for developing effective control measures. Furthermore, current exposure assessments often neglect the dynamic nature of population movement, typically relying on static data from census information. Efforts to improve these estimates through GPS studies that track real movements and modes of transport face challenges such as limited numbers of participants and privacy issues [7, 8, 13, 15]. For more targeted and effective policy decisions, more detailed data is required to capture the dynamic nature of air pollution and pedestrian mobility patterns in order to make more targeted and effective policy decisions. This approach enables more precise and timely strategies to mitigate air pollution impacts.

To address these multifaceted challenges, we propose a Multi-agent System (MAS) as a solution. This system is designed to better assess the impact of traffic emissions on local air quality and human health, taking into account pedestrian mobility patterns. Our approach improves the accuracy of exposure estimation and establishes a versatile platform for testing hypotheses and evaluating future scenarios. By allowing researchers to probe "what if" questions, this MAS illuminates the intricate behaviours of complex systems, offering a novel tool for exploring the potential impacts of the implementation of LEZ and beyond.

However, while several MAS studies have provided a detailed analysis of traffic patterns and emissions, they have focused primarily on changes in air quality levels and have not examined the positive health outcomes associated with such changes, i.e. increased life expectancy and reduced rates of low birthweight full-term births [6], or providing lack of the environmental impact of LEZ and traffic-related policies. Even among the few existing studies, like that of Ge and Polhill [5] and Shin and Bithell [14], more comprehensive approaches are still needed.

As a starting point, this workshop paper focuses on the development of an agent-based traffic simulation to assess the impact of the Glasgow LEZ scheme on traffic flows and emissions. The key research questions are outlined below:

- How have traffic patterns and air quality been affected following the enforcement of the LEZ?
- How can an agent-based model simulate pollutant emissions around the zone?

2 Methods

In this paper, we develop a proof-of-concept agent-based model. This approach enables us to simulate individual agents' behaviours and interactions within a defined environment, thereby illustrating potential dynamics and outcomes that could not be readily observed in the natural setting.

2.1 Study Area

The LEZ covers the city centre, which is bordered to the north and west by the M8 motorway, to the south by the River Clyde, and to the east by High St and Saltmarket (see Fig. 1 left). This area is approximately 4km². To simulate inbound and outbound traffic to the city centre, we included road networks from the M8, M77, and M74 motorways, as well as the A74, using the SUMO traffic simulator [9]. SUMO (Simulation of Urban MObility) allows vehicle agents to operate precisely on the road, rather than relying on rules at each junction, making it more accurate than other simulators such as NetLogo [16].

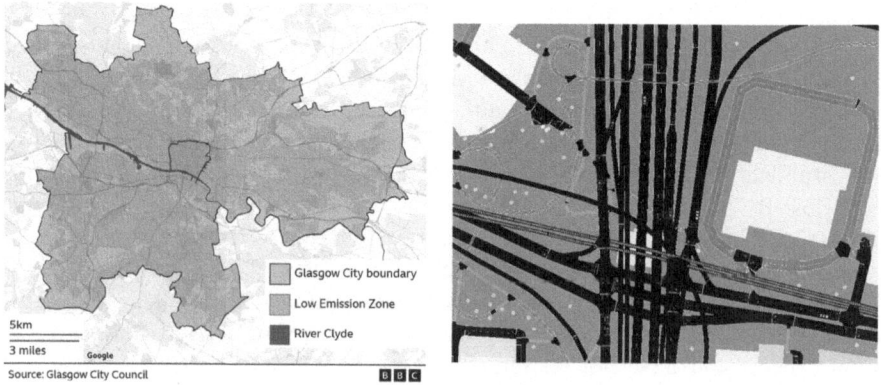

Fig. 1. Glasgow LEZ (left) and A snapshot of SUMO zoomed in Glasgow M8 motorway (right)

2.2 Agent-Based Traffic Simulation Using SUMO

We selected SUMO (Simulation of Urban Mobility) as our primary platform to ideally simulate an entire season and include vehicular traffic and pedestrian dynamics (although this paper only presents a single day result from the demo). SUMO is an open-source platform adept at managing extensive road networks within a continuous geographic realm. SUMO's primary use case is city traffic flow simulation and plotting individual vehicle routes.

We opted for SUMO due to technical and economic factors. SUMO's user-friendly graphical interface simplifies importing roadways in shapefile format, facilitating swift identification and rectification of disconnections. Road data is typically sourced from OpenStreetMap, encompassing nodes, links, and turn signals. These features saved significant time and technical effort during model construction.

Additionally, SUMO can collaborate with various other models, including emission models. iTETRIS, a model developed by the German government to reduce vehicle emissions, is one such example. Furthermore, since SUMO is written in C++ and Python, vehicle emissions can be calculated on High-Performance Computing such as the cluster located in our Unit at the University of Glasgow. Lastly, it's important to note that both SUMO and iTETRIS are freely available software packages that can be downloaded and used on Windows, Linux, or Macintosh operating systems.

2.3   Vehicles

To model non-resident vehicles, we plan to simulate buses, private vehicles, LGVs, and HGVs to assess traffic in and out of the city centre. However, the free SUMO version only allows the emission model for passenger cars only. Thus, for this paper we tested passenger cars. Vehicles that are registered as resident vehicles or belong to local businesses can travel to and from the LEZ boundary without issues. However, if the driver of a non-resident vehicle wishes to enter the LEZ, they must comply with the emissions standards, such as Euro 4 for petrol vehicles and Euro 6 for diesel vehicles. The table below provides an example of a passenger vehicle attribute (see Fig 1).

Table 1. An example of attributes of a vehicle agent

Type	Value (example)
Vehicle Type	Private Car
Make Year	2017
Fuel	Petrol
Euro	5
NOx	50
PMx	30
Origin	M8 northeast
Destination	Finneston
Current Road	Cathedral Street
Speed (mph)	18
Speed: Max	70
Arrive Time	"13:24 22/07/2023"
Counter (mins)	37

Vehicle agents that do not meet the Euro 4 unleaded or Euro 6 diesel standard will adapt to a new behaviour by assigning a new route as a destination. Once the new direction is assigned to these vehicles, the drivers must learn where to park for short periods of time and restart engines once they have re-entered the vehicle.

2.4   Emission Models

Our study concentrated on the vehicular emission models: HBEFA (The Handbook Emission Factors for Road Transport). HBEFA, pronounced as ha-bay-fa, offers pollution factors such as CO_2, CO, HC, NO_2, and PM_x across vehicle categories and fuel types. Once the model's traffic has been verified (e.g. vehicles are not bumping into people or teleporting somewhere randomly), we plan to incorporate the UK Department for Environment, Food and Rural Affairs (DEFRA) standards into our model. Another potential option is GRAL (Graz Lagrangian Model) [12], which accounts for urban meteorological conditions and morphology.

3   Demo

In this demo, we present the current state of emission functions over a simulated 1,500-second period (approximately equivalent to one day). The model explores how these emissions might change if parts of the network were blocked. Although the model is still in its testing phase and vehicles are heading randomly, the results clearly illustrate significant congestion as vehicles accumulate on the network (see Fig. 2).

Figure 3 shows the preliminary emissions output for the roads at each time step (in seconds) within the study area. The initial peak is attributed to the presence of only a few vehicles at the start of the simulation. After approximately 50 s, the traffic volume appears to stabilise towards the end of the simulation.

For all three pollutants, there is a clear oscillation in emissions over time. While the patterns vary between pollutants, the troughs in the oscillation coincide with instances when vehicles come to a standstill.

For example, suppose a car is planning a 10 km trip around the Glasgow LEZ and is travelling at an average speed of 50 km/h.

The time taken to travel 10 km is:

$$Time(hours) = \frac{Distance(km)}{speed(km/h)} = \frac{10}{50} = 0.2 \tag{1}$$

Convert time to seconds:

$$0.2\,h \cdot 3600 = 720\,s \tag{2}$$

Total emissions:
Emissions (mg) = Rate (mg/s) · Time (s) =

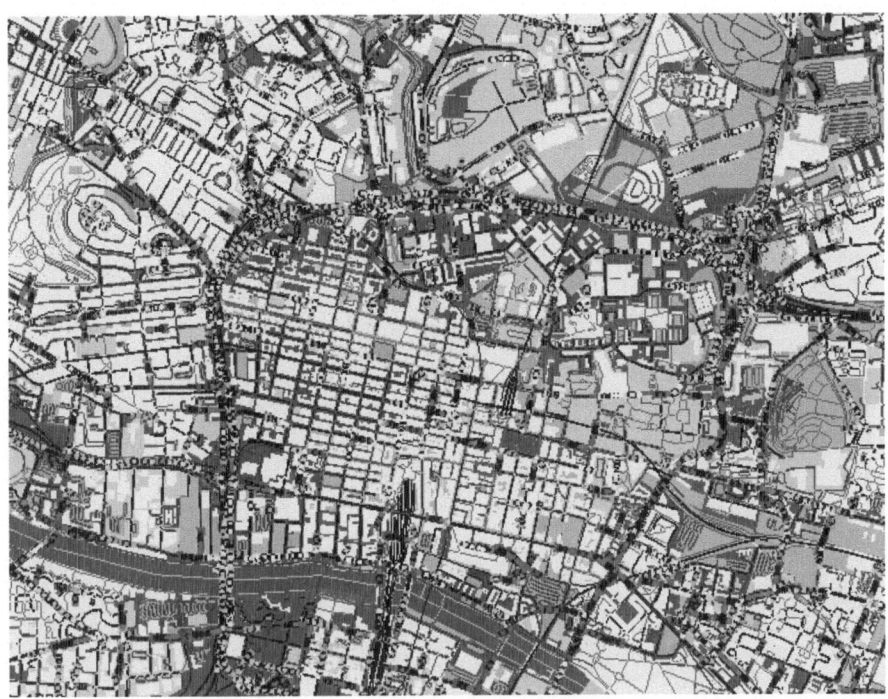

Fig. 2. SUMO zoomed in on Glasgow Central. Most of the congestion is on the outskirts of the M8 motorway. The colour represents the vehicle's speed, with the blues and greens being those currently moving, while the oranges and reds are stationary or moving very slowly.

$$1000\,mg/s \cdot 720\,s = 720,000\,mg \tag{3}$$

This analysis shows that a vehicle travelling 10 km emits approximately 720 grams of CO_2, equivalent to 72 g per km. Under these conditions, vehicles in Glasgow would generally meet the EU standard of 95 g CO_2/km based on 2020–2024 period (see here for details). However, this calculation represents only one example. For instance, another vehicle travelling less than 5 km could exceed the 95 g CO_2/km threshold.

Limitations. Currently, the model is based on a random traffic flow pattern so it does not mimic the realistic traffic patterns around central Glasgow. Also, we have a very nonoptimised traffic flow after 2000 s of the simulation, where most of the cars are on minor roads (street level) cannot move forward. Improved results are expected as we calibrate the traffic patterns specific to the city's Low Emission Zone (LEZ) and explore a variety of scenarios. We are using the Compass IoT traffic dataset (visit the Consumer Data Research Centre UK website) for calibration.

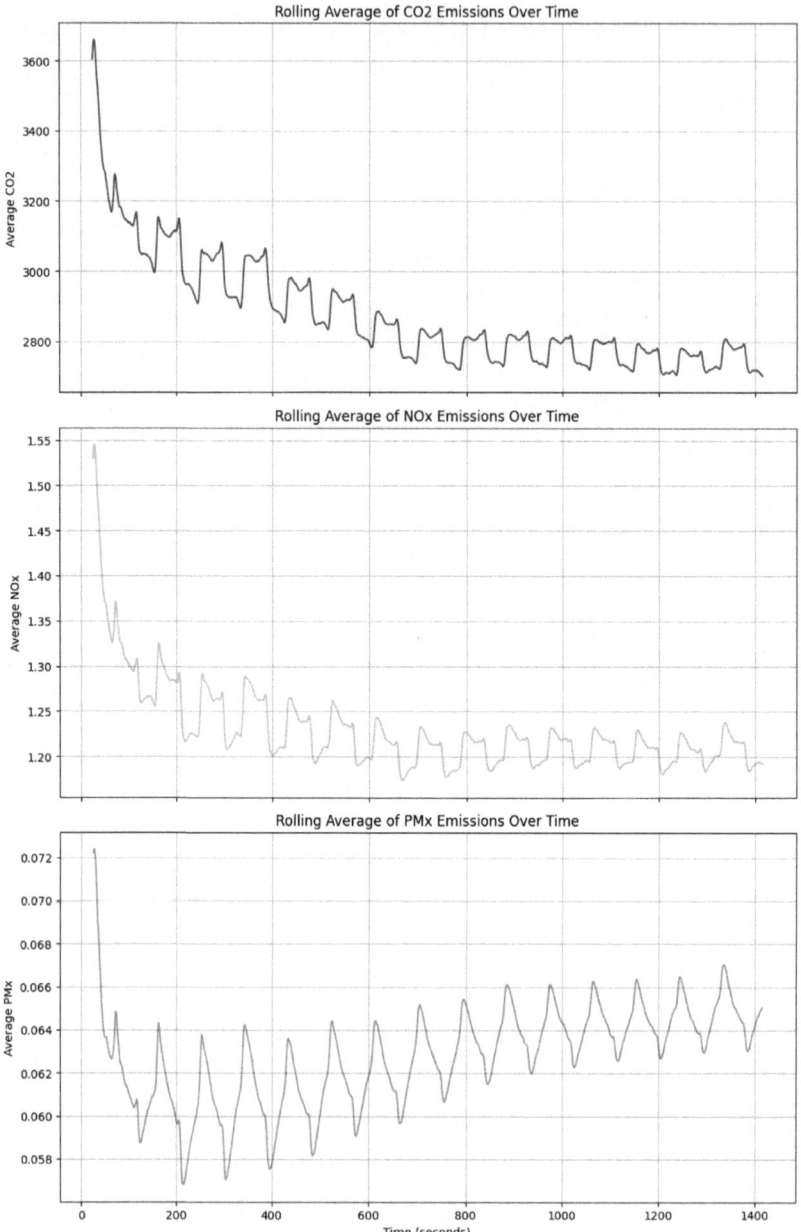

Fig. 3. Emission per time step from 1000 vehicles (rolling average). Note not all thousand vehicles appear in the simulation until around 50–100 s after the start of the simulation.

Another issue encountered is the occurrence of road collisions, partly due to the absence of pavements on certain lanes. Finally, vehicles 'teleport' within the simulation due to edge effects. These issues highlight areas for improvement to increase the accuracy and reliability of the model.

4   Conclusion

Our study investigates the impact of Glasgow's Low Emission Zone (LEZ) on traffic flow, traffic-related emissions, and pedestrian exposure to air pollution. Using an agent-based traffic simulation model built on SUMO, which is still work-in-progress, we were able to capture the dynamics of vehicle and pedestrian movements within the LEZ, including emission oscillations over time and the effects of road network disruptions. These results highlight the need for further calibration of traffic patterns and enhanced road infrastructure, such as pavements, to reduce collision risks and improve pedestrian safety.

Future work will address these challenges by incorporating realistic traffic datasets, refining pedestrian mobility models, and testing diverse policy scenarios to improve the accuracy and applicability of the simulation.

5   Data and Code Availability

The data and codes for this project are all openly available via the following GitHub repository: https://github.com/dataandcrowd/GlasgowLEZ_SUMO.

References

1. Air Quality Expert Group: Non-exhaust emissions from road traffic
2. Beevers, S.D.: Traffic management strategies for emissions reduction : recent experience in London, pp. 27–39 (2016)
3. Cambridgeshire City Council: Air Pollution in Cambridgeshire, pp. 1–44 (2016). https://doi.org/10.1016/B978-0-08-092605-6.50007-7
4. David, N., Don, G.: An integrated agent-based framework for assessing air pollution impacts. J. Environ. Prot. **2012** (2012)
5. Ge, J., Polhill, J.G.: Exploring the combined effect of factors influencing commuting patterns and co2 emissions in aberdeen using an agent-based model. J. Artif. Soc. Soc. Simul. **19**(3), 11 (2016). https://doi.org/10.18564/jasss.3078, http://jasss.soc.surrey.ac.uk/19/3/11.html
6. Host, S., Honoré, C., Joly, F., Saunal, A., Le Tertre, A., Medina, S.: Implementation of various hypothetical low emission zone scenarios in greater paris: assessment of fine-scale reduction in exposure and expected health benefits **185**, 109405. https://doi.org/10.1016/j.envres.2020.109405, https://linkinghub.elsevier.com/retrieve/pii/S001393512030298X
7. Hwang, Y., Lee, K.: Contribution of microenvironments to personal exposures to PM10 and PM2.5 in summer and winter. Atmospheric Environ. **175**, 192–198 (2018). https://doi.org/10.1016/j.atmosenv.2017.12.009, http://www.sciencedirect.com/science/article/pii/S1352231017308269

8. Liang, L., Gong, P., Cong, N., Li, Z., Zhao, Y., Chen, Y.: Assessment of personal exposure to particulate air pollution: the first result of City Health Outlook (CHO) project. BMC Public Health **19**(1), 711 (2019). https://doi.org/10.1186/s12889-019-7022-8

9. Lopez, P.A., et al.: Microscopic traffic simulation using sumo, pp. 2575–2582. IEEE

10. Min, K.D., et al.: Association between exposure to traffic-related air pollution and pediatric allergic diseases based on modeled air pollution concentrations and traffic measures in Seoul, Korea: a comparative analysis. Environ. Health **19**(1), 6 (2020). https://doi.org/10.1186/s12940-020-0563-6

11. Nyhan, M., et al.: "exposure track" - The impact of mobile-device-based mobility patterns on quantifying population exposure to air pollution. Environ. Sci. Technol. **50**(17), 9671–9681 (2016). https://doi.org/10.1021/acs.est.6b02385

12. Romanov, A.A., et al.: Graz lagrangian model (GRAL) for pollutants tracking and estimating sources partial contributions to atmospheric pollution in highly urbanized areas **11**(12), 1375, publisher: MDPI

13. Sanchez, M., et al.: Personal exposure to particulate matter in peri-urban India: predictors and association with ambient concentration at residence. J. Exposure Sci. Environ. Epidemiology **30**(4), 596–605 (2020). https://doi.org/10.1038/s41370-019-0150-5, http://dx.doi.org/10.1038/s41370-019-0150-5

14. Shin, H., Bithell, M.: TRAPSim: an agent-based model to estimate personal exposure to non-exhaust road emissions in central seoul **99**, 101894. https://doi.org/10.1016/j.compenvurbsys.2022.101894, https://linkinghub.elsevier.com/retrieve/pii/S0198971522001387

15. Steinle, S., et al.: Personal exposure monitoring of PM2.5 in indoor and outdoor microenvironments. Sci. Total Environ. **508**, 383–394 (2015). https://doi.org/10.1016/j.scitotenv.2014.12.003, http://dx.doi.org/10.1016/j.scitotenv.2014.12.003

16. Wilensky, U.: NetLogo

17. Williams, C.: Air pollution from busy traffic and its 'grim reaper' effect on glasgow communities https://www.glasgowlive.co.uk/news/glasgow-news/glasgow-air-pollution-grim-reaper-18798721

MABS Education

Teaching Agent-Based Modeling for Simulating Social Systems – A Research-Based Learning Approach

Fabian Lorig[1,2](✉) [iD], Michael Belfrage[1,2] [iD], and Emil Johansson[1,2] [iD]

[1] Department of Computer Science and Media Technology, Malmö University, Malmö, Sweden
[2] Internet of Things and People Research Center, Malmö University, Malmö, Sweden
`fabian.lorig@mau.se`

Abstract. Existing courses on agent-based modeling and simulating (ABMS) are mainly aimed at doctoral students and many modelers have acquired their ABMS skills by teaching themselves. This paper reports and reflects on the development of an undergraduate course on ABMS of social systems. It presents a problem-based approach to teaching ABMS of social systems, the Integrated Learning Outcomes (ILOs), and the course structure. This paper discusses the constructive alignment of the syllabus, presents the results from the course evaluation, and draws conclusions for further editions of the course. Rather than proposing how such courses should be structured, we discuss the feasibility of the pursued research-based learning approach. Our goal is to inspire other researchers and teachers to develop similar courses, to encourage the establishment of a general curriculum, and to promote ABMS in undergraduate education.

Keywords: Agent-based Social Simulation · Teaching · Education · Problem-based Learning · Inquiry-based Learning

1 Introduction

Agent-based Modeling and Simulation (ABMS) of human behavior and social phenomena is increasingly applied across different disciplines. Lately, its potential to facilitate policy modeling and decision support has gained attention. During the Covid-19 crisis, ABMS have been used to simulate the consequences and effects of different non-pharmaceutical interventions on society [1]. Also in other areas, e.g., land-use, fishery, agriculture, and transportation, increasing collaborations between agent-based modelers and policy actors and an interest in ABMS of social systems can be observed [2].

In academia, agent-based modelers have diverse backgrounds, and many have acquired their ABMS skills by teaching themselves. This might be due to a lack of standard teaching materials, training programs, and integration into higher education programs and curricula [3]. Some ABMS courses exist, e.g., summer schools and short tutorials, but these are mainly designed for doctoral students. The participants of these courses often have diverse (non-technical) backgrounds and attend the training to receive

J. Thompson and I. Stankov (Eds.): MABS 2024, LNAI 15583, pp. 39–53, 2025.
https://doi.org/10.1007/978-3-031-88017-9_4

a first introduction to ABMS, which they need for their PhD projects [4]. Many are committed to using ABMS and actively search for suitable courses, either because they self-identified the need to take a course on this topic or because they were recommended to do so by their doctoral supervisors.

In undergrade education, the situation is different. ABMS is rarely part of the higher education curriculum and, if existing, stand-alone (elective) courses are offered. Also, undergraduate students do not usually have the intrinsic desire to learn about ABMS as many have neither heard of this method nor face issues that benefit from or suggest the use of ABMS. What makes teaching of ABMS at undergraduate level challenging is the method's inherent interdisciplinarity, required prior knowledge, skills, and understanding (e.g., in computer science, behavioral science, and statistics), and the diverse range of ABMS applications (e.g., in biology, ecology, and economics) [5].

To promote the advancement of ABMS, to establish ABMS as a well-trusted tool for knowledge generation and in decision support, and to train the next generation of agent-based modelers, we believe undergraduate education needs to be advanced. We developed an elective undergraduate course on *Agent-based Modeling for Simulating Social Systems*. The goal of this course is for the students to develop both knowledge and skills on the use of ABMS as tool and research method for analyzing social systems and phenomena. We pursue an inquiry-based learning approach, which is a learning form that actively engages students in the learning process, encourages a high level of participation, and promotes the development of problem-solving strategies.

This paper reports and reflects on the development of this course and on the experiences from teaching its first edition. We present a problem-based approach to teaching ABMS of social systems, the Integrated Learning Outcomes (ILOs), and the course outline we pursued. We discuss the constructive alignment of the syllabus, present results from the course evaluation, and draw conclusions for coming editions.

The course is hosted at Malmö University, Sweden, and was given for the first time in Spring 2023 as an elective self-study course. The presented syllabus is by no means intended as a silver bullet to teaching ABMS. Yet, we believe that sharing of and reflecting on experiences from educating the next generation of modelers will inspire other teachers and facilitate the establishment of a curriculum.

The paper is structured as follows: Sect. 2 gives a brief introduction to research-based learning and an overview of practices in teaching ABMS. In Sect. 3, we present the ILOs and the outline of the course and Sect. 4 describes the constructive alignment. In Sect. 5, we present results from the course evaluation and draw conclusions in Sect. 6.

2 Background

2.1 Research-Based Learning

Integrating research and teaching in higher education can enhance the students' learning experience and create a stimulating and productive learning environment [6]. It also facilities the shift from *teacher-centered education*, a traditional approach, where the teacher is in charge of learning and where students are passively being presented knowledge, towards *student-centered learning*, where the teacher functions as a facilitator (*teacher as partner*), embracing active learning [7, 8].

In contrast to traditional teacher-centered education, which still is common practice in many technical disciplines, research-based approaches put the students in charge of their own learning by letting them independently carry out research as part of the course. This can promote a more symmetric teacher-student relationship and improve the students' learning experience. Moreover, practically experiencing the entire research process also facilitates the students' deeper understanding in contrast to, for instance, lying focus on memorizing facts as in traditional teacher-centered education [9].

Healey [10] argues that the active involvement achieved through research-based learning positively affects the students' depth of learning and understanding. However, they also emphasize that the development of research-based curricula is a demanding task for teachers as new approaches need to be developed that facilitate collaboration between students and teachers.

What is challenging when implementing a research-based teaching approach is to ensure *pedagogic resonance* between the learning design (i.e., the course design), the learning experience (i.e., learning activities), and the learning discipline (i.e., subject-specific traditions) [11]. Edwards et al. [6] emphasize that the integration of teaching and research does not happen on its own and that, depending on the practices and traditions of the discipline, the one or the other part might be neglected. To achieve pedagogic resonance, it needs to be made clear for the students how this learning strategy relates to their studies and to cultivate expectations regarding roles and activities.

There exist different terms describing similar active learning strategies with the goal of enabling students to acquire knowledge through actively identifying and exploring real-world questions in a research-inspired way. These include, among others, *inquiry-based learning, research-based learning, problem-based learning, case-based learning*, and *evidence-based learning* [12]. In this article, we use the term *research-based learning* to refer to this group of education strategies.

2.2 Teaching Agent-Based Modeling and Simulation

In ABMS, which is often applied by researchers and in a scientific context, a strong connection between research and education seems inevitable. This connection is further endorsed by the fact that existing textbooks and courses are often tailored towards researchers and that there is a lack of standard teaching materials [13].

There are some scientific publications that discuss challenges in teaching ABMS and report on courses and pedagogical approaches. Macal & North [14] present different ABMS teaching strategies that they have successfully applied. They also propose different course outlines and suitable demonstration models. Lorig et al. [4] reflect on the learning outcomes and their experiences from a PhD tutorial on ABMS for policy making. During the Covid-19 pandemic, Bijak et al. [15] report on their experiences from teaching ABMS in an online setting and provide a blueprint for designing and running a course. There are also teaching reports from the earlier days of social simulations, e.g., Thorngate [16] and Carvalho [17], which present how specific simulation frameworks can be used. An example for teaching ABMS in a cross-disciplinary settings is presented by Augustijn et al. [18], who teach ABMS and machine learning.

There are specialized courses from universities and research institutions, including online courses, e.g., ACTiSS[1], as well as on-site university courses, for instance, at Linköping University[2] (SE), TU Delft[3] (NL), and the Central European University[4]. There exist different ABMS summer schools that take place regularly and primarily address doctoral students, e.g., the BEHAVE summer school[5], the ESSA summer school[6], and the MISS-ABMS summer school[7]. Finally, courses exist on commercial platforms such as Coursera[8] and ComplexityExplorer[9]. These are just some examples of existing courses, and more courses exist, most of which are not given at regular intervals. A study by de Mesquite et al. revealed that even though a greater number of simulation courses exist, only around 26% of the analyzed courses include ABM [19].

3   Intended Learning Outcomes and Outline

The proposed course consists of six Intended Learning Outcomes (ILOs), which define what students will be able to do upon successfully completing this course. According to the Swedish Higher Education Ordinance [20] (Ch 6 Sect 4), the ILOs are defined based on six forms of knowledge: *knowledge & understanding*, *competence & abilities*, and *evaluation abilities & approach*. For formulating ILOs according to the different knowledge dimensions and levels of understanding, we used Blooms knowledge taxonomy [21], which provides examples of measurable active verbs (*action words*).

After completing this course, the student should be able to:

(knowledge & understanding)

   ILO1) explain basic concepts in agent-based modeling and simulation
   ILO2) describe how ABM can be used for simulation of social systems

(competence & abilities)

   ILO3) implement agent-based models using simulation frameworks
   ILO4) plan and perform simulation experiments

(evaluation abilities & approach)

   ILO5) discuss the suitability of applying agent-based modeling and simulation
   ILO6) evaluate and interpret simulation results

---

[1] https://actiss-edu.eu/ (accessed Nov 2024).

[2] https://liu.se/en/education/course/771a22 (accessed Nov 2024).

[3] https://ocw.tudelft.nl/courses/agent-based-modeling-of-complex-adaptive-systems-basic/ (accessed Nov 2024).

[4] https://courses.ceu.edu/courses/2023-2024/agent-based-models (accessed Nov 2024).

[5] https://behavelab.org/behave-summer-school/ (accessed Nov 2024).

[6] http://www.essa.eu.org/event-type/summer-school/ (accessed Nov 2024).

[7] http://www.agropolis.org/miss-abms/ (accessed Nov 2024).

[8] https://www.coursera.org/projects/abm-netlogo (accessed Nov 2024).

[9] https://www.complexityexplorer.org/courses/146-introduction-to-agent-based-modeling-summer-2022 (accessed Nov 2024).

To support the students in achieving these ILOs, the course combines different working forms and learning strategies to ensure the constructive alignment. The course consists of three consecutive modules, which build on each other (see Fig. 1). Each module consists of a combination of carefully linked theoretical and practical learning elements, enabling the students to actively engage with practical exercises and examples, to promote learning though investigation, and the self-development of skills. To assess the students' learning progress, the course is examined through formative assessment (three written assignments) at the end of each module and summative assessment (a final project), which are mandatory and need to be successfully completed to pass the course.

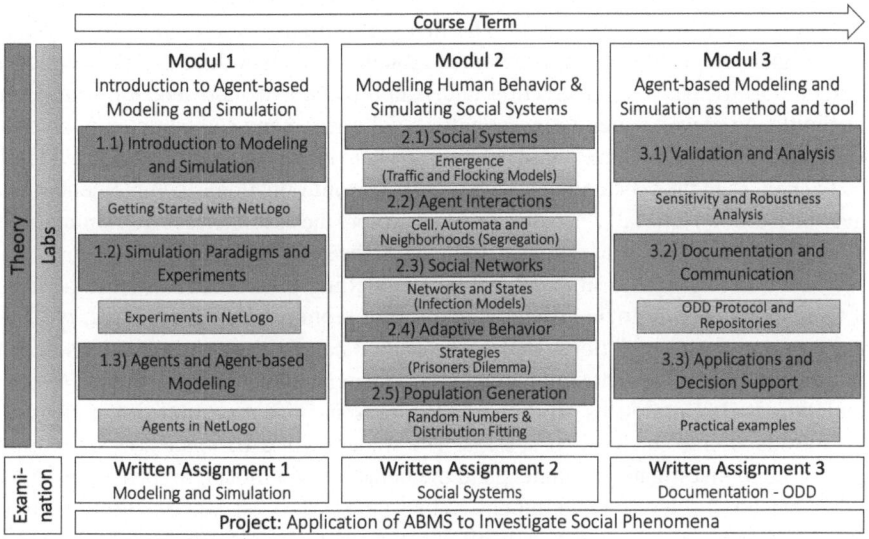

Fig. 1. Structure of the course: The course consists of three consecutive modules, each of which consists of theoretical (dark grey) and practical (light grey) learning elements. Each module is complemented by a written assignment (white), and a comprehensive final project (white).

The practical part (labs) is based on NetLogo[10], which is an open-source and free-to-use multi-agent programing language and modeling environment. It is well suited for beginners but is also widely used by more advanced users in academic settings. We have chosen NetLogo for this course as it provides a variety of ready-to-use models, does not require previous programming skills, and allows for easily building visualizations and user interfaces to execute the model.

Even though ABMS course literature is sparse, there are some valuable textbooks to support student learning. We have chosen to combine chapters from different textbooks to provide optimal support. Two books that provide an intuitive and hand-on introduction to ABM are Railsback & Grimm [22] and Wilensky [23]. Both books use plenty example models in NetLogo to introduce core ABM concepts. To complement the simulation perspective, we used the books from Law [24] and Banks et al. [25], as well as

---

[10] https://ccl.northwestern.edu/netlogo/index.shtml (accessed Nov 2024).

Montgomery [26] to introduce experimentation. Finally, the social science perspective is provided by Gilbert & Troitzsch [27] and Robins [28]. In addition to these textbooks, different research articles are used in specific modules and submodules.

3.1 Module 1: Introduction to Agent-Based Modeling and Simulation

Module 1 introduces ABMS and assumes that the student does not have any prior knowledge on modelling and simulation. It pursues a problem-based constructivist approach, presenting and motivating interesting issues and questions that can be addressed using ABMS and promoting ILOs 1 and 4. After completing the module, the student is able to explain basic concepts in ABMS and to design simulation experiments.

Module 1 consists of three parts. The first part introduces simulations as a method to investigate and understand how complex systems work as well as the basic concepts of modelling focusing on abstraction and simplification. It motivates why modeling and simulation is well suited to investigate social phenomena and complex population dynamics using a real-world example of rabies, where individual-based models evidently lead to changes in the vaccination strategy [29]. This introduction is complemented by a hands-on NetLogo tutorial, where the students explore the user interface, run simulations, and modify model parametrizations using a wolf-sheep-predation model.

When teaching ABMS, it is debatable if modelling or simulation should be introduced first. To keep it novice friendly, and to not require programing skills, we have chosen to start with simulations. Hence, the second part focuses on simulations in general and introduces different simulation paradigms related to ABM, e.g., discrete-event simulation. It also introduces experimentation, presents different strategies, and gives a brief introduction to stochastic processes. The student will experience how simulations can be used to investigate and understand the behavior of a model, to then learn how to modify existing or develop own models. The second lab is on experimenting with the wolf-sheep-grass model, to systematically investigate the model's behavior.

Finally, the third part introduces different types of intelligent agents and the concept of ABMS to model complex behavior in artificial populations. A special focus is on what makes ABMS different from other modelling paradigms and when it is most beneficial to use ABMS. In the third lab, the student will also implement an own model. The exercises are designed as a code-along, where we encourage the students to try to solve the exercises on their own, yet, code examples are also provided that can be used.

The module is then concluded by a written assignment, where the different elements from the first module are combined, i.e., executing and understanding an existing model, developing a conceptual model, and implementing a model in NetLogo.

3.2 Module 2: Modeling Human Behavior and Simulating Social Systems

Module 2 focuses on achieving ILOs 2 and 3, and the student acquires an understanding of how ABMS can be used to simulate social systems and skills for modeling human behavior. Accordingly, this module focuses on situating the techniques taught in module 1 to applications in social systems. The first lecture introduces how different disciplines have contributed to and constituted the research area of ABMS, which also benefits the student orientation and how the ABMS could be situated in their field.

The introduction to modeling and simulation from module 1 allows us to introduce ABMS from a computational social science perspective. By introducing the weak notion of agency, opportunity structures, and institutional constraints of social systems, the goal is to enable the student to delineate and model social systems in society. To anchor these modelling concepts scientifically, the following lecture presents scientific theory about causality, methodological individualism, and experimental methodology. This is followed by concepts associated with simulation and the instantiation of models across time like interdependence, curve linear functions, and emergence. The submodule's lab relates to emergent phenomena, e.g., flocking of Boids and traffic congestion.

The second submodule presents agent sensing and types of agent interaction, followed by an introduction to sub-models, neighborhoods, and cellular automata which we investigate in the second lab. We also analyze Schelling's segregation model to provide practical examples of feedback effects and path dependence. The third submodule focuses on social networks in ABMS. We introduce the mathematical motivation necessitating the use of graphs, different types of networks, network theories, centrality measurements, and network typologies. The lab introduces the student to contagion problems and applies the SIR model to investigate the propagation of viruses.

The fourth submodule introduces the theory of adaptive behavior and modeling concepts like fidelity and realism. The goal is to introduce the student to the challenging task of modeling heterogenous human-like decision-making. We provide a brief introduction to microeconomic theory and utility functions, which is complemented by examples of two agent-architectures, a need-based model (ASSOCC [30]) and a comprehension and adoption model (associative diffusion [31]). The lab presents the extended version of the prisoner's dilemma where the student explores and develops different behavioral strategies. The last sub-module presents different approaches and tools used in population generation for realistic agent populations and demonstrates how the student can use NetLogo for pseudo-random number generation.

3.3 Module 3: Agent-Based Modeling and Simulation as Method and Tool

The third and final module introduces concepts related to applying ABMS as a research method and targets ILOs 5 and 6. This module assumes that the student has a fundamental understanding of how to develop ABMs of social systems from the first two modules. Module 3 is shorter and aims to give an overview of challenges and approaches to apply models rather than an in-depth understanding of any specific method. It does not include any labs, and the written assignment does not include any coding.

First, the module covers Verification and Validation (V&V). Since the student does not necessarily have a programing background, the V&V part includes basic bug-testing techniques and code hygiene. Next, the concepts of uncertainty analysis, sensitivity analysis, and robustness analysis are introduced. Finally, it discusses methods for quantitative and qualitative model validation. After completing this submodule, students can describe why V&V of models is important, know methods for performing V&V, and understand challenges that arise when doing so.

The second submodule concerns communication of agent-based models, and in particular using the ODD protocol [32]. In addition to aiding modelers in the communication of their models, the protocol is a useful tool for conceptualizing and structuring models during the model creation phase [22], thus being valuable for the student even if they do not seek to publish their models in the future. The third module's written assignment consists of creating an ODD description of a specific model. Not only does creating an accurate and comprehensive ODD description require a thorough understanding of both the protocol and the explained model; it also requires the student to understand principles such as emergence, adaptation, and stochasticity, which are all included in the protocol.

Finally, we present and discuss real-world applications of ABMS, e.g., in modeling, logistics, epidemiology, agriculture, evacuation modeling, and criminology. A model that has been used in real-world decision-making is given as an example for each of the covered domains. The reason for concluding the course with this submodule is so that the student will be able to see the connections between what they've learned and what is being done in state-of-the-art models and research, facilitating it for students to find ways to apply and further develop their knowledge outside of the course.

3.4 Examination: Final Project

As intended by the research-based learning approach, it is the goal of this course to cover the entire inquiry process. The different steps were part of the individual modules and in the final project, we put these together to one coherent approach. Accordingly, the goal of the final project is to identify a problem that can be analyzed using ABM, to describe how simulation can be used to investigate and better understand this problem, and to develop a conceptual model that described how a simulation could work, i.e., agent types, stochastic processes, input and output data, model components etc.

Following the example of scientific symposia, the students have to submit a scientific poster, a short report, and a description of their (conceptual) model. An example of a poster submitted by one of the students is shown in Fig. 2.

4 A Research-Based Approach to Teaching ABMS

The research-based teaching approach we pursue in this course is inspired by different approaches for engaging undergraduate students in inquiry proposed by Healey and Jenkins [33] (see Fig. 3). It consists of four steps, that provide the students with theories, techniques, and research they require to independently conduct own simulation studies.

Starting with a *research-oriented* perspective, students develop necessary skills and techniques in a problem-based fashion. This includes ABMS theories and a hands-on introduction to working with simulation frameworks. Following, a *research-led* perspective is chosen, where students learn about current research topics and different applications of ABMS, using case studies. As a third step, a *research-tutored* perspective is employed, where students actively find and critically discuss relevant research. The course concludes with a *research-based* perspective, where the student actively conducts research and applies their acquired knowledge in an own simulation study.

This approach facilitates the steep learning curve, which results from the fact that the students will start the course without any prior ABMS knowledge. Then, after only 6–8 weeks of studying, the students are encouraged to identify and formulate an own

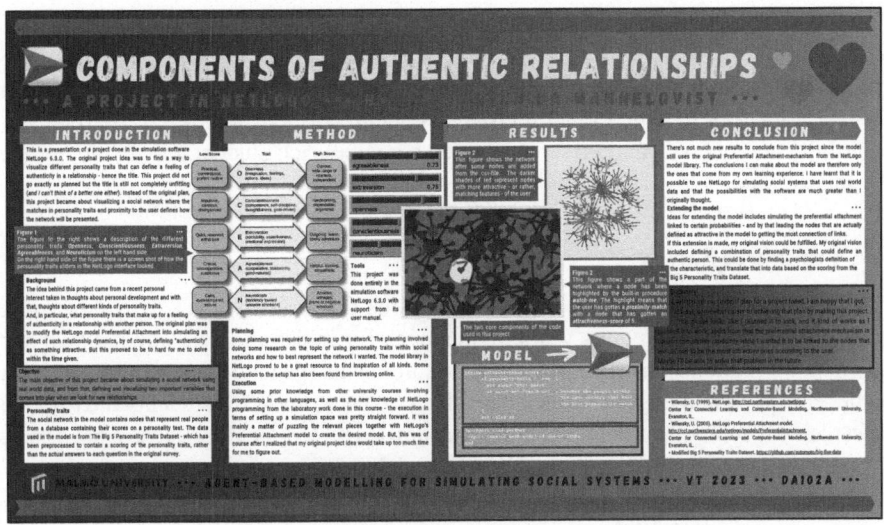

Fig. 2. Example of a student's final project poster submissions. Linn Veronica Mannelqvist developed an ABMS of social networks to investigate authenticity in relationships.

research question that can be addressed using ABMS, to develop a suitable model for addressing this question, and through this to actively conduct ABMS research.

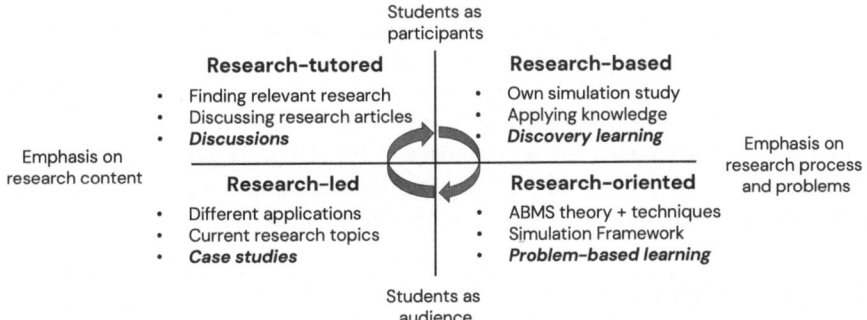

Fig. 3. Engaging students in research and inquiry, based on Jenkins & Healey [33].

5   Student Surveys and Course Evaluation

As part of the first edition of the course, two student surveys[11] have been conducted. The first survey was sent out four weeks before the start of the course with the goal to get to know the students, to better understand their expectations, their preferred learning styles, and their previous knowledge. The second survey was sent out at the end of the

---

[11] The questionnaires used for the surveys and the students' replies are shared upon request.

course to assess the students' study experience, to analyze to what extent the students reached the ILOs, to give them the possibility to express their feedback, and to help us to further develop the course. Both surveys were conducted using an online tool, where link were sent out by email to all registered students. In both surveys, the participants were fully anonymous, and the system made sure that each student only could answer the survey once.

5.1 Pre-course Survey

This course was given as an elective course for the first time, which is why there were no experiences from previous years. It was open for registration for any national and international students that fulfil the course requirements (general entry requirements for higher education and English proficiency). Thus, to get to know the students and to better meet their expectations, needs, and previous knowledge, we decided to send a pre-course survey to all 43 registered students. We received 28 replies (65%).

When asked why they have chosen to take this course now, 43% replied that this course sounded most interesting amongst the elective course, 36% attend the course voluntarily, 11% do research in this area, 11% take it in preparation for another course or program, and 4% need it for their job. Regarding the students' previous experiences and knowledge, 18% have attended courses on modeling and simulation, 14% on social systems and human behavior, and 11% on ABM. 71% of the respondents have not attended courses on these topics before. 18% of the respondents have previous used some simulation framework (e.g., Arena and AnyLogic) and none had used NetLogo before.

Finally, the students were asked which learning strategies work best for them. 54% want to work alone on assignments, 7% in groups, and 39% in a mixture of individual and group work. Even though the course was announced as 7.5 ECTS points[12] with a duration of 10 weeks (i.e., 20 h per week), 39% of the students replied that they plan to spend between 5–10 h per week on the course, 21% plan to spend 10–15 h, and 32% plan to spend 15–20 h. The results of the remaining questions that were asked in both the pre-course and the end-of-course survey are shown in Sect. 5.3.

5.2 End-of-Course Survey

After the course, we did a second survey to evaluate the students' learning. This survey focused on how well the learning strategy worked, to what extent the students reached the ILOs, and what can be improved for next year's edition. Of the 43 initially registered students, 36 actively used the learning platform, 23 completed the first assignment, 14 the second assignment, and 13 the third assignment and the final project. This corresponds to 36%[13] of the initially active students successfully completing the course.

---

[12] According to the European Credit Transfer and Accumulation System (ECTS), one full-time academic year corresponds to 60 ECTS credits. In Sweden, 1 ECTS credit corresponds to 26.66 h of student workload.

[13] Sweden does not charge tuition fees, which leads to a high number of students (ca. 34%) that only study elective courses, e.g., alongside their job. We assume this is a contributing factor to the relatively high dropout rates, which are similar to other elective courses.

First, the students were asked to what extent they have achieved each of the ILOs on a scale from 1 (very low extent) to 5 (very high extent). ILO1 was achieved to a high (4 of 5) or very high extent (5 of 5) by 92% of the students, ILO2 by 92%, ILO3 by 92%, ILO4 by 85%, ILO5 by 62%, and ILO6 by 54%. For none of the ILOs, any of the students assessed their achievement with less than 3 of 5.

85% say that the working methods and activities supported their learning to a high or very high extent and 85% state that the examination form allowed them to demonstrate how well their have achieved the ILOs to a high extent. When asked how many hours they spent on the course, 8% of the students spent 15–20 h a week, 38% spent 10–15 h, 31% spent 5–10 h, and 23% less than 5 h. The requirements to pass the course were assessed as "just right" by all students expect for one.

5.3 Student Development Throughout the Course

Some questions were part of both questionnaires to assess the students' development by comparing their knowledge, skills, and mindset before and after the course. As the questionnaires were anonymous, we cannot evaluate the students' individual development. Still, conclusions regarding the students' learning progress can be drawn.

Before the start of the course, the estimation how many hours the students will spend on the course was evenly scattered between 5 up to 20 h. After the course, however, we see that most students spent less hours than they initially thought with the majority spending between 5 to 15 h a week.

In the pre-survey, most students stated that they want to learn about ABM (82%) and social systems (75%), followed by simulation and human behavior (both 64%). After the course, the number of students that have learned about the different aspects to a high or very high extent is 100% for ABM, 83% for social systems, 67% for human behavior, and 92% for simulation. 83% state they have learned about the link between these aspects to a high or very high extent (see Fig. 4).

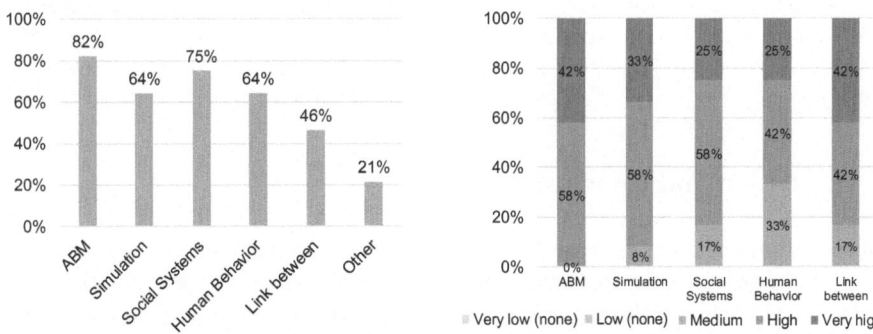

Fig. 4. Answers from the pre-course (left; N = 28) and post-course (right; N = 13) surveys. What do you want to learn from the course? / What have you learned from the course?

The anticipated context of use for what they have learned in this course shifted. Potential use in research (from 11% to 38%), other courses (11% to 31%), decision support (29% to 46%), and work (32% to 46%) have increased significantly. Both teaching (11% to 15%) and not having use of it (29% to 31%) only increased slightly.

When comparing the students' skills before and after the course, we see an increase in programing (39% to 53% with high and very high knowledge), data analysis (from 36% to 46%), modelling (11% to 70%), analyzing human behavior (14% to 46%), and analyzing social networks (32% to 62%). Acquiring programming and data analysis was not explicitly goal of this course, thus, this increase might serve as an indicator which students successfully completed the course. Another possible explanation is that the labs help the students to improve these skills.

Regarding ILO fulfillment, we also see significant increases. The high and very high ability to explain what ABMS is increased from 14% to 92%, the use of ABMS to analyze social systems from 4% to 77%, the ability to implement ABMs from 11% to 62%, to design simulation experiments from 14% to 62%, to assess the suitability of applying simulations for a given question from 7% to 70%, and the ability to analyze simulation results from 7% to 62%. While around 60% to 90% stated that they had very low to low knowledge on the different ILOs in the post course survey, no student assessed their own knowledge on any of the ILOs as low or very low after the course.

Before the start of the course, students evenly estimated they will spend between 5 up to 20 h. After the course, however, we see that most students spent less hours than they initially thought with the majority spending between 5 to 15 h a week.

When comparing the study experience, we see a shift towards more senior students from before to after the course. Both questionnaires were sent out during the same term, so that we expected similar distributions. Instead, we see an increase in those students that have studied for 10 or more terms from 21% to 38% as well as a decrease in the group students that have studied for 5–6 terms from 46% to 38%. The other groups are almost unchanged, from which we can infer drop-out students.

Finally, we repeated the questions about the study discipline. Here we see a significant increase in natural science (14% to 46%), humanities (14% to 23%), and culture/design (4% to 8%) but also a decrease in social sciences (14% to 8%), economics (21% to 0%), and law (4% to 0%). The ratio of students from technology was the same (68% and 69%).

6   Discussion and Conclusions

This paper presents and discusses our experiences from developing an undergraduate course on ABMS of social systems. Rather than proposing how such a course should be structured and held, we discuss the feasibility of the research-based learning approach we pursued. Our goal is to inspire other researchers and teachers to develop similar courses, to address the lack of full-time courses, to establish a general curriculum, and to promote ABMS in undergraduate education.

We could observe a broad interest in ABMS of social systems, given the variety in students' backgrounds. Yet, it seems that most students chose the course due to specific aspects that are covered. Students have discovered the wide application range of ABMS, where we saw an increase in potential uses in research, work, and decision support after the course. A remaining challenge is to convey practical skills, i.e., model development, experimentation, and result analysis. Almost all students assess that they have gained high knowledge on what ABMS is and when it can be applied, however, only two-thirds assess their practical ABMS skills as high. Finally, we observed a drop-off of students with backgrounds in economics, law, and social sciences, disciplines, where ABMS can be of great value, yet, we can only speculate about the reasons.

The benefits resulting from the research-based approach include a high motivation and engagement from the students, shifting their role in the course from consumers to knowledge creators. It also promotes a symmetric teacher-student relationship and a deeper understanding of the subject rather than memorizing facts. Yet, there are also challenges related to this learning approach. This includes that the approach requires a high intrinsic motivation of the learners due to self-study approach and because of the is comparatively steep learning. Because of this, it is also more challenging for the teachers to identify students that need support in their learning. Since there was no preceding course that was run using another learning approach, it is difficult to assess to what extent the choice of research-based learning contributed to the students' success.

The students were positive about the structure of the course and commented that they enjoyed the different approach compared to other courses they take. Still, we also received the wish for live lectures and more practical sessions with other students, as a complement to the self-study parts of the course.

Acknowledgements. This work is partially supported by the Wallenberg AI, Autonomous Systems and Software Program – Humanities and Society (WASP-HS), funded by the Marianne and Marcus Wallenberg Foundation. We would also like to thank Linn Veronica Mannelqvist for her excellent work and for allowing us to show and publish her poster.

References

1. Lorig, F., Johansson, E., Davidsson, P.: Agent-based social simulation of the Covid-19 pandemic: a systematic review. J. Artif. Soc. Soc. Simul. (JASSS) **24**, 5 (2021)
2. Belfrage, M., Lorig, F., Davidsson, P.: Simulating change: a systematic literature review of agent-based models for policy-making. In: 2024 Annual Modeling and Simulation Conference (ANNSIM), pp. 1–13 (2024)
3. Janssen, M.A., Alessa, L.N., Barton, M., Bergin, S., Lee, A.: Towards a community framework for agent-based modelling. J. Artif. Soc. Soc. Simul. **11**, 6 (2008)
4. Lorig, F., Vanhée, L., Dignum, F.: Agent-based social simulation for policy making. In: Chetouani, M., Dignum, V., Lukowicz, P., Sierra, C. (eds.) Human-Centered Artificial Intelligence, pp. 391–414. Springer International Publishing, Cham (2023)
5. Macal, C.M., North, M.J.: Toward teaching agent-based simulation. In: Proceedings of the 2010 Winter Simulation Conference, pp. 268–277. IEEE (2010)
6. Edwards, C., et al.: Cultivating student expectations of a research-informed curriculum: developing and promoting pedagogic resonance in the undergraduate student learning pathway. In Developing the Higher Education Curriculum Research-based Education in Practice, Edited by Brent Carnell and Dilly Fung. Dev. High. Educ. Curric. Res.-Based Educ. Pract. Ed. Brent Carnell Dilly Fung. (2017)

7. Tabak, I., Baumgartner, E.: The teacher as partner: exploring participant structures, symmetry, and identity work in scaffolding. In: Investigating Participant Structures in the Context of Science Instruction, pp. 393–429. Routledge (2014)
8. Murphy, L., Eduljee, N.B., Croteau, K.: Teacher-centered versus student-centered teaching: preferences and differences across academic majors. J. Eff. Teach. High. Educ. **4**, 18–39 (2021)
9. Khuana, K., Khuana, T., Santiboon, T.: An instructional design model with the cultivating research-based learning strategies for fostering teacher students' creative thinking abilities. Educ. Res. Rev. **12**, 712–724 (2017)
10. Healey, M.: Linking research and teaching to benefit student learning. J. Geogr. High. Educ. **29**, 183–201 (2005). https://doi.org/10.1080/03098260500130387
11. Polias, J.: Pedagogical resonance: improving teaching and learning. 42–49 (2010)
12. Michael, J.: Where's the evidence that active learning works? Adv. Physiol. Educ. **30**, 159–167 (2006). https://doi.org/10.1152/advan.00053.2006
13. Collins, A., Petty, M., Vernon-Bido, D., Sherfey, S.: A call to arms: standards for agent-based modeling and simulation. J. Artif. Soc. Soc. Simul. **18**, 12 (2015)
14. Macal, C.M., North, M.J.: Successful approaches for teaching agent-based simulation. In: Taylor, S.J.E. (ed.) Agent-Based Modeling and Simulation, pp. 271–290. Palgrave Macmillan UK, London (2014). https://doi.org/10.1057/9781137453648_13
15. Bijak, J., et al.: Teaching a modeling process: reflections from an online course. In: Winter Simulation Conference, WSC 2021, Phoenix, AZ, USA, December 12–15, 2021, pp. 1–12. IEEE (2021)
16. Thorngate, W.: Teaching social simulation with Matlab. J. Artif. Soc. Soc. Simul. **3** (2000)
17. Carvalho, J.: Using agentsheets to teach simulation to undergraduate students. J. Artif. Soc. Soc. Simul. **3**, 2 (2000)
18. Augustijn, E.-W., Kounadi, O., Kuznecova, T., Zurita-Milla, R.: Teaching agent-based modelling and machine learning in an integrated way. GeoComputation (2019)
19. de Mesquita, M.A., da Silva, B.C., Tomotani, J.V.: Simulation education: a survey of faculty and practitioners. In: 2019 Winter Simulation Conference, pp. 3344–3355. IEEE (2019)
20. Swedish Council for Higher Education: The Higher Education Ordinance (1993:100) (2024). https://www.uhr.se/en/start/laws-and-regulations/Laws-and-regulations/The-Higher-Education-Ordinance/
21. Krathwohl, D.R.: A revision of bloom's taxonomy: an overview. Theory Pract. **41**, 212–218 (2002). https://doi.org/10.1207/s15430421tip4104_2
22. Railsback, S.F., Grimm, V.: Agent-based and Individual-Based Modeling: A Practical Introduction. Princeton University Press (2019)
23. Wilensky, U., Rand, W.: An Introduction to Agent-Based Modeling: Modeling Natural, Social, and Engineered Complex Systems with NetLogo. Mit Press (2015)
24. Law, A.M.: Simulation Modeling and Analysis. McGraw-Hill, Dubuque (2014)
25. Banks, J.: Discrete-Event System Simulation. Pearson, Harlow (2014)
26. Montgomery, D.C.: Design and Analysis of Experiments. John Wiley & Sons Inc, Hoboken, NJ (2013)
27. Gilbert, G.N., Troitzsch, K.G.: Simulation for the Social Scientist. Open University Press, Maidenhead, England; New York, NY (2005)
28. Robins, G.: Doing Social Network Research: Network-based Research Design for Social Scientists. SAGE Publications Ltd. (2015). https://doi.org/10.4135/9781473916753
29. Eisinger, D., Thulke, H.-H., Selhorst, T., Müller, T.: Emergency vaccination of rabies under limited resources – combating or containing? BMC Infect. Dis. **5**, 10 (2005)
30. Dignum, F., et al.: Analysing the combined health, social and economic impacts of the coronavirus pandemic using agent-based social simulation. Mind. Mach. **30**, 177–194 (2020)

31. Goldberg, A., Stein, S.K.: Beyond social contagion: associative diffusion and the emergence of cultural variation. Am. Sociol. Rev. **83**, 897–932 (2018)
32. Grimm, V., et al.: The ODD protocol for describing agent-based and other simulation models: a second update to improve clarity, replication, and structural realism. J. Artif. Soc. Soc. Simul. **23**, 7 (2020)
33. Jenkins, A., Healey, M.: Undergraduate research and international initiatives to link teaching and research. CUR Q. **30**, 36–42 (2010)

MABS Applications

KEMASS: Knowledge-Enhanced Multi-agent simulation for energy Scheduling Support

Guillaume Muller[1]($\boxtimes$)(ID), Somsakun Maneerat[2](ID), and Alan Adamiak[2]

[1] Mines Saint-Etienne, Institut Henri Fayol, Saint-Etienne, France
guillaume.muller@emse.fr
[2] EDF, R&D, SEQUOIA, Lab Paris-Saclay, Palaiseau, France
somsakun.maneerat@edf.fr

Abstract. The transition to decentralized energy distribution, where any node can function as a consumer and/or producer, presents challenges in the design and testing of control algorithms, particularly in maintaining production. The existing energy scheduling model, assuming uniformity, struggles to capture the unique dynamics and constraints of individual production units. This paper introduces KEMASS, a method and system for generating a Multi-Agent System using Ontologies and Knowledge Graphs to tailor optimization algorithms for power plants. Implemented in a specific energy production valley, KEMASS closely simulates the actual system, optimizing energy schedule while considering local constraints. Although not yet a complete Digital Twin for Energy Scheduling Support, KEMASS, with its dynamic Knowledge Graphs and Ontologies, is more adaptable to evolving into one compared to other systems. The use of Knowledge Representation technologies makes it suitable for various applications.

Keywords: Multi-Agent System · Ontology · Knowledge Graph · Multi-Agent System Engineering · Simulation · Energy · Real-world scenarios

1 Introduction

The energy sector is shifting from conventional to renewable energy sources, leading to a decentralized production landscape with diverse stakeholders. This transition to a complex and decentralized energy system (a.k.a. SmartGrid) poses growing challenges in balancing supply and demand on electrical grids, as well as in designing management and optimization algorithms for companies in the energy sector [17,21].

The existing forecasting and optimization model for electricity production, assuming uniformity across facilities, fails to capture sector dynamics and constraints unique to each production unit. Disparities between production schedules and actual capacities require frequent adjustments and human verification.

© The Author(s), under exclusive license to Springer Nature Switzerland AG 2025
J. Thompson and I. Stankov (Eds.): MABS 2024, LNAI 15583, pp. 57–69, 2025.
https://doi.org/10.1007/978-3-031-88017-9_5

The optimization algorithm needs customization for each power plant type, and coordinating diverse units involves interacting with multiple systems. Engineers designing new SmartGrid algorithms need to test them under various conditions (e.g. extreme cases). However, as the actual energy system must remain in production, testing on it is nearly impossible.

If the engineers would have a Digital Twin (DT) of the system at their disposal, they would be able to set up such specific scenarios, run some simulations, collect data, select the best solutions and apply them directly to the actual system, when required. In this paper, we propose KEMASS, a methodology/implementation, that generates a Multi-Agent System (MAS) based on Knowledge Representations (KR) of the various components of the actual system, represented with Ontologies[1] and Knowledge Graphs[2].

Choosing MAS as the digital twin in the DT is straightforward given SmartGrid's decentralized structure and autonomous elements. Employing KR allows energy engineers to express their expertise seamlessly, ensuring interoperability among diverse facility agents and facilitating interaction with future external systems [21].

The paper is organized as follows: Sect. 2 discusses related works and limitations of current approaches; Sect. 3 details the ontology construction and the KEMASS system; Sect. 4 presents the results from running the MAS for an energy production in a French valley; and Sect. 5 discusses KEMASS's strengths, weaknesses, and potential extensions.

2   Related Works

There are three main approaches to mixing Multi-Agent Systems and Knowledge Representations in the literature:

- **External once-and-for-all generation of the MAS**: [7,8,15] provide external means to generate the MAS, once and for all, from the KRs (e.g. a toolchain that generates code, or Protégé plugins for MAS mapping).
- **External specifications for the MAS**: [24] uses KGs to formulate the specifications of the system. The description of the agents is "external", like an API. The representation of the system can be manipulated, e.g. by the agents themselves, to "understand" how to call a service or communicate with another entity, but they do not need to know how the service/agent will do its job.

---

[1] An Ontology is a formal and explicit specification of a shared conceptualization. It is a way of representing knowledge in a machine-readable format that can be understood by both humans and machines. Ontologies define *concepts* and *categories*, as well as their *properties* and *relations* [13].

[2] Knowledge Graphs (KGs) are some sort of instantiation of an Ontology on a set of individual data points. A KG is a graph-based database that represents knowledge in a structured and semantically rich format. It is a way of organizing and representing data that allows for more efficient and effective processing of information [13].

- **Runtime generation of Agents**: [4,11,19] generally deploy special "constructor" agents/services in the MAS platform/language, which use the representation of the system, to generate agents, from the KRs, at runtime. In this strategy, it is important to model the "internal" functioning of the agents (i.e. "executable code"), in order to completely instantiate the agents. The approach allows for some level of verification of the MAS specifications.

A true Digital Twin [10] requires connections in **both directions** between the physical system and the virtual one. The first approach lacks the possibility to have a backward connection from the running virtual system to the physical system. The second approach lacks the internal representation of the agents' functioning, thus does not completely implement the connection from the physical system to the virtual system. Only the third approach is opened to the creation of a true DT. We thus focus mostly on this approach.

To further describe the connection between KR and MAS, we will rely on the "Vowels" paradigm [2]), that identifies five components in MAS: **A**gents, **E**nvironment, **I**nteractions, **O**rganization, **U**ser, and discuss the use of KRs at each of these levels.

Some works, such as [6,9,23] employ KRs at the **A**gent level for reasoning, while others use them at the **I**nteraction level as a "common language", to smooth inter-agent communications [8,16,22,23], particularly as a means of interoperability between different sources of information [1,3]. As emphasized in [16], these uses of KRs in MAS are related. Indeed, if **A**gents communicate using KRs, they already manipulate elements on which they can reason. Thus, it is reasonable to design the reasoning process of these agents based on the same KRs [16]. Moreover, if **A**gents' reasoning is based on KRs, they are most probably already manipulating concepts from the **O**rganization/**E**nvironment levels, in their KRs. The prospect of designing the complete MAS using these KRs is thus in close reach. At best, papers in the literature are using Ontologies as the unique Knowledge Representations to describe the actual system. Ontologies can represent the structure of the system, including classes and their relations. However, Ontologies do not provide sufficient detail to fully instantiate an agent, including configurations/values of its properties, from real-world data, a task at which Knowledge Graphs excel. This is the main contribution of KEMASS, our model. This is also, the specific means that will allow the MAS to communicate back with the physical system, thus opening the door the generation of an actual DT.

3 Methodology

The objective of KEMASS is to automatically generate Multi-Agent Systems (MAS) from energy system descriptions using Knowledge Representations. The paper specifically focuses on developing a tool to assess the feasibility of production schedules for hydropower plants in a French valley, taking into account both local and global constraints. The modeling incorporates absolute timesteps, each lasting 30 min, to ensure synchronous agent operation.

Our methodology comprises two components: (1) domain representation and (2) automatic MAS generation, as illustrated in Fig. 1.

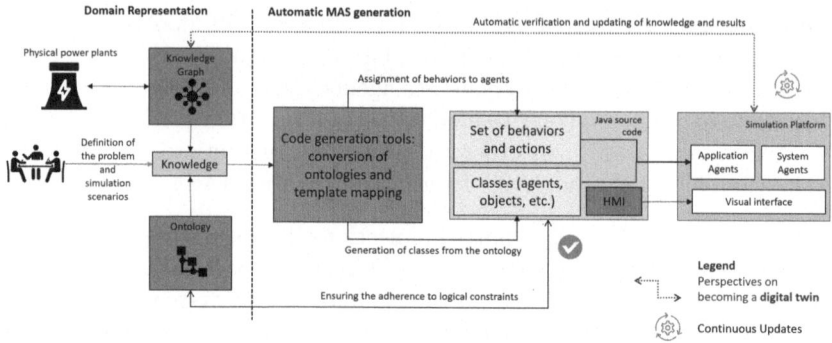

Fig. 1. The Methodology for automatically Generating a Multi-Agent System platform from Knowledge Representation and its prospective evolution into a Digital Twin.

3.1 Domain Representation

Domain knowledge is represented through the creation of an Ontology and a Knowledge Graph (Fig. 2). These Knowledge Representation elements serve as a resource generator for our Multi-Agent Systems simulation. An example of this is the transformation of the blue classes in the Hydropower Ontology into MAS agents.

Agents and their organization: Local constraints modeled at the **Production facility**[3] include unit activation times, operating duration adjustments, capacities, water flow rates, and power output. This Production facility entity is a subclass of **Physical object**, a broad category covering shared characteristics between **Production facilities** and **Reservoirs**.

At the regional level, constraints revolve around the spatial position of **Physical Objects** in a **Valley**, impacting flow, operational capacity, and collaboration sequencing.

At a global scale, a **Programming Entity** manages production scheduling of **Productions Facilities** in **Valleys**, specifying time slots and power demand for each.

Agent behaviors and interactions: Agent behaviors are intricately integrated into the template linked to ontology classes, providing flexibility for modeling within our implementation. The dynamic interaction and coordination among all agents, as conditioned by the ontology, are illustrated in Fig. 3. The MAS starts with the reactive agent **Programming Entity** transmitting daily production schedules for coordination to each **Production facility** agent. The **Production facility**, in turn, initiates actions through a Finite State Machine (FSM) encompassing main states of the plant: *shutdown*, *restart*, and *production*. In the *shutdown* state, the agent remains inactive, periodically checking for a need to resume activity. During the *restart* phase, the agent takes some duration to find the best operating point based on instant water flow before

---

[3] Bold text marks Agent names.

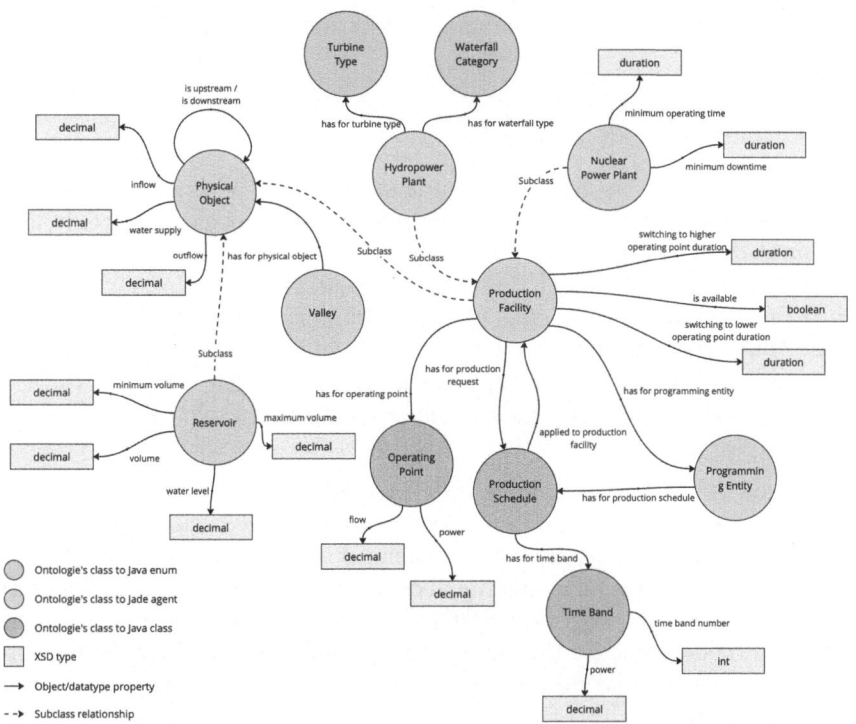

Fig. 2. The Hydropower Ontology and its corresponding Java mapping components.

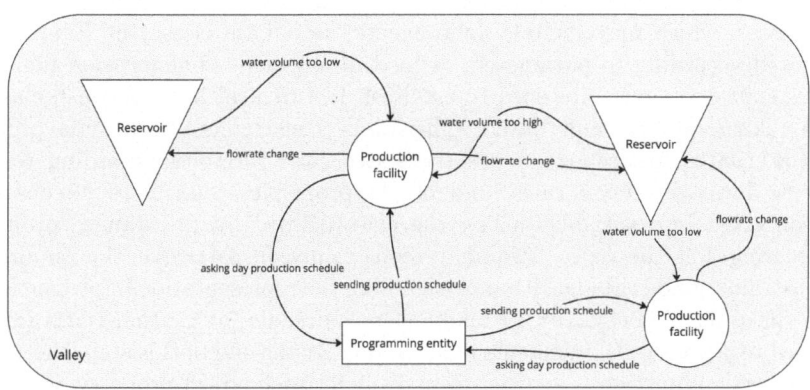

Fig. 3. Exchanged messages between agents.

resuming *production*. The agent communicates flow information to upstream and downstream agents classified as **Physical objects**, records production and flow rates, conveys efficiency information during operating point changes, and notifies of *shutdown*. **Reservoir** agents update water volume, adjust inflow/outflow based on messages, and introduce random adjustments in the inflow with a cyclic behavior.

3.2   Automatic MAS generation

This section presents the KEMASS methodology, for generating and running a Multi-Agent System from Knowledge Representation implemented as Ontologies and Knowledge Graphs.

The section centers on the KR-to-MAS conversion methodology, which occurs in two primary stages involving three programmatic objects known as (see Fig. 4): *Main* (the algorithm launcher), *ConstructAgent*, and *ClassBuilder*. The initial step involves the generation of Java classes from the ontology, while the second step instantiates Jade agents from a knowledge graph.

Generation of Agents' Class from Ontologies

The first phase of our KR-to-MAS conversion algorithm is class creation. Managed by an agent builder, this stage combines the loading of ontologies into memory and the generation of functional classes through the *ClassBuilder* utility. Ontology files are converted into RDF4J[4] models. The ontologies are split into two RDF4J models, one for the main ontology, and the second for the imported ones. This solution is paving the way for the selection of relevant classes in the construction of the final MAS.

Conversion rules: After initializing the algorithm, the constructor agent relies on a class dedicated to conversion, the *ClassBuilder*. The *ClassBuilder* plays a crucial role in translating ontological concepts into executable Java code. Ontology classes, which may include Jade agents, Java base classes or Enums, are generated according to parameters defined in a specific configuration file. The `SubClassOf` properties are used to establish hierarchical links between classes, while taking into account Java's inheritance constraints. Data type properties (`owl:DatatypeProperty`) are translated into variables according to the XSD to Java conversion rules, and object properties (`owl:ObjectProperty`) are converted into variables, using the class defined by the "range" property (`rdfs:range`) as the type. Cardinality constraints, in particular the "minimum 1" constraint, guide the algorithm by signaling the representation of properties in the form of lists (`ArrayList`). Finally, class indivuals (`owl:classIndividual`) are used to represent the elements of an Enum. At the end of this step, the ontology conversion function is invoked recursively for each object property, when the variable's type class is defined in external ontologies. For more detail of the KR-to-MAS conversion, see Table 1 in the Appendix.

Templates to create source code: Once all the classes have been parsed, the algorithm uses the Apache FreeMarker template engine to translate the data into Java code. Each class refers to a template determined by information in the configuration file, facilitating the conditional integration of class-specific

---

[4] https://www.rdf4j.org/.

elements. Behaviors, currently coded manually in additional template, are then integrated into the generated Java source code.

Once the source files have been written[5], the Java Compiler receives a path module containing only the classes and functions of the dependencies essential to the program. In this way, the MAS agents are compiled and the class names passed on to Jade.

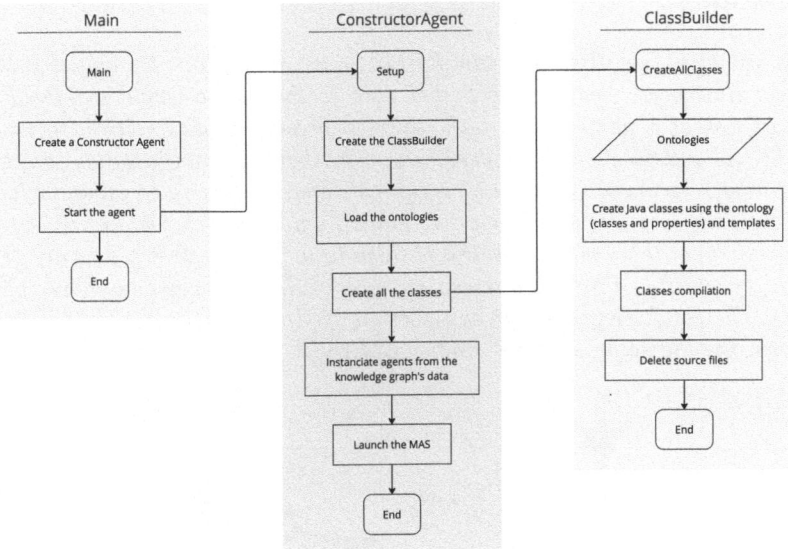

Fig. 4. The agent generation process.

Agent Instantiation from Knowledge Graph

This step involves executing specific SparQL queries overseen by the constructorAgent. The queries provide the flexibility to integrate constraints customized for the specific context. In this study, limitations are applied to select only a single valley.

Initially, (1) a query is executed to obtain the complete list of classes present in the knowledge graph. Then, (2) for each identified class, a new query is formulated to retrieve all related properties, including their cardinality where applicable. When properties exhibit cardinality, a specialized function is invoked to significantly reduce the number of queries, ensuring optimal performance. Each property is then stored in a Java variable of type Map, where the variable name serves as the key and its type as the value. If the property corresponds to a

---

[5] The source codes are compiled in a single batch, a strategy designed to anticipate the potential problems of circular dependencies common when using ontologies.

class, a third SparQL query is deployed to retrieve all the elements necessary for agent instantiation. (3) The instantiation phase concludes by launching an agent of the appropriate class and passing the Map of variables as an argument. This latter is used at the agent's startup to initialize its variables using the *Reflection API*. This pragmatic approach ensures efficient agent initialization, taking into account context-specific dependencies in the Multi-Agent System (MAS).

4   Results

Note on the Results: *We ran KEMASS on data from an actual valley in France. However, releasing the actual data to the public would put the Energy Grid at risk of a dangerous attack, as such precise data is critical to its functioning. As a consequence, we designed an artificial hydraulic valley (see Fig. 5) containing 1 reversible plant (which can consume electricity to pump water back into its reservoir) and 5 hydroelectric plants, among which two are run-of-river. To complement these plants, we linked them to their respective reservoirs. To add to the complexity of the representation, one of the reservoirs has two upstream plants. The results presented in this section are based on the artificial valley, but demonstrate the same behavior from KEMASS.*

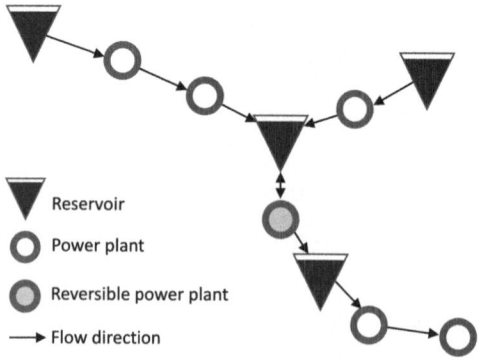

Fig. 5. Fake valley structure

Simulations record what happens at every moment, such as the amount of electricity produced or the quantity of water in the reservoirs. These recordings help us observe how things unfold during the simulation.

An evaluation was conducted on the simulation's compliance with the production schedule, focusing on water flow and produced energy. The graphs (see Fig. 6) revealed that the simulation was not perfectly aligned with the production schedule due to specific rules considered by our simulator, such as the required wait times after certain changes. Our field experts clarified that this observation aligns with the daily routine of the energy company, which often involves manually adjusting production scheduling. This highlights the role of our simulator, which acts as a digital tool to verify the compliance of the production schedule with local rules.

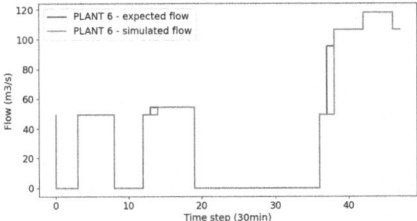

Fig. 6. Verification of a power plant's flow regulation compliance with its production schedule.

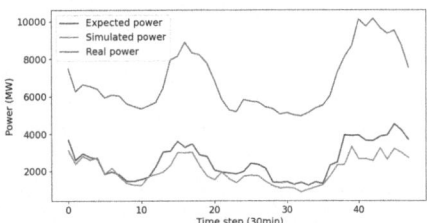

Fig. 7. Comparison between daily hydroelectric production in France among RTE data, our simulation output, and production scheduling.

To validate our approach, we analyzed simulation results, focusing on assessing their resemblance to reality in terms of produced energy. Due to limited access to actual factory data, a direct comparison at the agent level (Production Facility) was not feasible. However, partial validation was achieved at the aggregated level by comparing simulated total hydroelectricity production in France, considering all modeled Production Facilities, with data from RTE's ÉCo2mix[6]. The simulation results align with similar trends, despite producing less electricity than reported by RTE (see Fig. 7). Expert discussions confirmed the realism of these results, highlighting that the energy company manages only a subset of power plants (around 16%), while others face unmodeled local constraints in our simulator, thus maintaining coherence with real-world constraints in KEMASS's results.

5   Discussions

Based on the results, KEMASS demonstrates significant potential as confirmed by domain experts and its ability to simulate a trend similar to real-world produced energy data. However, it is acknowledged to be in the early stages of development, and its validation has been partial. This section delves into both current limitations and ongoing enhancements.

Validation: KEMASS involved testing it in three scenarios: using real and synthetic data from a hydropower valley and data from another valley, resulting in realistic outcomes. However, further validation is essential using a broader range of real-world data in terms of volume and variety to enhance its reliability and

---

[6] https://odre.opendatasoft.com/explore/dataset/eco2mix-national-tr/information/?disjunctive.nature.

robustness. Works like [5,12,14] provide relevant approaches in this direction. To ensure the scalability of KEMASS, we are expanding our current Knowledge Representations by incorporating additional energy types (e.g., nuclear plants) and incorporating data from diverse valleys simultaneously. Additionally, we plan to extend the application of KEMASS to different domains, such as healthcare or manufacturing, for comprehensive validation.

Internal Agent model: The modeling of agent behaviors is currently expressed through a template system based on Finite State Machines (FSM). Despite its utility, this approach lacks the expressiveness inherent in a Turing Machine, consequently affording agents a less generic foundation for potential evolution, as articulated by domain experts. To address this limitation, our objective is to advance a more expressive and user-friendly representation of agent behaviors, leveraging Knowledge Representation. The adaptability of our system to this evolutionary trajectory is underpinned by its KR-to-MAS auto-generate system. [18] provides an interesting alternative approach automatic generation of agent behavior models that we would benefit integrating in KEMASS.

Time representation: Our application uses absolute time with a fixed timestep, which may not fit other applications. KEMASS can be modified to fit different time scales (even at the same time), by simply ensuring: 1) message ordering in agents and 2) correct time scale representation(s) in Knowledge Representation. It could also be favorable to adapt the temporality model of [20] in KEMASS.

Full Digital Twin: KEMASS's main contribution is the combined use of Ontologies and Knowledge Graphs, allowing for a potential feedback loop between the virtual and physical systems (as shown in Fig. 1). This could enable KEMASS to generate a full Digital Twin of any system. To ensure bidirectional data flow, KEMASS's `ConstructorAgent`(s) would need to update KRs and MAS as changes occur.

6   Conclusion

This paper introduced KEMASS, a methodology that enables the generation and execution of a Multi-Agent System directly from a domain representation, leveraging the synergy of Ontologies and Knowledge Graph.

Our application of KEMASS to an electric production scenario in a hydraulic valley yielded promising initial findings, demonstrating the system's ability to closely replicate the outcomes of the original system and pinpoint disparities in production scheduling versus actual plant capacity.

However, for comprehensive validation, KEMASS necessitates further testing with additional empirical data. Two ongoing improvements to KEMASS are underway: (i) refining agent behaviors using a more complex and flexible system based on Knowledge Representation, and (ii) establishing synchronization between MAS updates and KR updates to achieve an authentic Digital Twin of the modeled system.

While initially designed for energy scheduling support, we have meticulously crafted each process to be as generic as possible. As a result, our system holds potential for application in diverse domains that can be represented with Ontologies and Knowledge Graphs, requiring minimal modifications.

Acknowledgments. We express our gratitude to EDF R&D, encompassing the AIDA project for their crucial support and the Direction Optimisation Amont Aval Trading (DOAAT) for their use case, conducted within the EDL project framework, which has greatly influenced our research. We look forward to continued exploration within the EDL project, and we are grateful to all involved.

Disclosure of Interests. Somsakun Maneerat and Alan Adamiak work for EDF company and have received granting from the AIDA project framework.

NOTE. *Generative AI tools have been used in the process of creating this paper, for writing improvements (ChatGPT) and for finding additional references (ResearchRabbit).*

Appendix

Table 1. The mapping between XSD types and Java objects.

Type XSD	Type Java
anyURI	java.net.URI
base64Binary	String
boolean	boolean
byte	byte
date	java.time.LocalDate
dateTime	java.time.LocalDateTime
dateTimeStamp	java.time.LocalDateTime
dayTimeDuration	java.time.Duration
decimal	double
double	double
duration	java.time.Duration
ENTITIES	ArrayList<String>
ENTITY	String
float	float
gDay	int
gMonth	java.time.Month
gMonthDay	java.time.MonthDay
gYear	java.time.Year
gYearMonth	java.time.YearMonth
hexBinary	String
ID	String
IDREF	String
IDREFS	ArrayList<String>
int	int

Type XSD	Type Java
integer	int
language	String
long	long
Name	String
NCName	String
negativeInteger	long
NMTOKEN	String
NMTOKENS	ArrayList<String>
nonNegativeInteger	long
nonPoritiveInteger	long
normalizedString	String
NOTATION	String
positiveInteger	long
QName	String
short	short
string	String
time	java.time.LocalTime
token	String
unsignedByte	int
unsignedInt	long
unsignedLong	long
unsignedShort	int
yearMontDuration	java.time.Duration

References

1. Cranefield, S., Purvis, M., Nowostawski, M., Nowostawski, M., Hwang, P.: Ontologies for interaction protocols. In: Tamma, V., Cranefield, S., Finin, T.W., Willmott, S. (eds.) Ontologies for Agents: Theory and Experiences, pp. 1–17. Birkhäuser Basel (2005)
2. Demazeau, Y.: From interactions to collective behaviour in agent-based systems. In: European Conference on Cognitive Science, vol. 95 (1995)
3. Dikenelli, O., Erdur, R.C., Özgür Gümüs: Seagent: a platform for developing semantic web based multi agent systems. In: AAMAS '05, Proceedings of the fourth international joint conference on Autonomous Agents and MultiAgent Systems, pp. 1271–1272. Association for Computing Machinery, New York, NY, USA (07 2005)
4. Donzelli, C., Kidanu, S.A., Chbeir, R., Cardinale, Y.: Onto2MAS: an ontology-based framework for automatic multi-agent system generation. In: 12th International Conference on Signal-Image Technology & Internet-Based Systems (SITIS), pp. 381–388. IEEE (01 2016)
5. Drchal, J., Čertický, M., Jakob, M.: Data driven validation framework for multi-agent activity-based models. In: Gaudou, B., Sichman, J.S. (eds.) Multi-Agent Based Simulation XVI, pp. 55–67. Springer International Publishing, Cham (2016)
6. Drozdowicz, M., et al.: Ontologies, agents and the grid: an overview. Parallel Distrib. Grid Comput. Eng. 117–140 (2009)
7. Freitas, A., Bordini, R.H., Meneguzzi, F., Vieira, R.: Towards integrating ontologies in multi-agent programming platforms. In: IEEE/WIC/ACM International Conference on Web Intelligence and Intelligent Agent Technology, WI-IAT 2015, Singapore, December 6–9, 2015 - Volume III, vol. 3, pp. 225–226. IEEE (2015)
8. Freitas, A., Bordini, R.H., Vieira, R.: Designing multi-agent systems from ontology models. In: Weyns, D., Mascardi, V., Ricci, A. (eds.) Engineering Multi-Agent Systems - 6th International Workshop, EMAS 2018, Stockholm, Sweden, July 14–15, 2018, Revised Selected Papers. Lecture Notes in Computer Science, vol. 11375, pp. 76–95. Springer International Publishing (2018)
9. Freitas, A., et al.: Semantic representations of agent plans and planning problem domains. In: Dalpiaz, F., Dix, J., van Riemsdijk, M.B. (eds.) Engineering Multi-Agent Systems: Second International Workshop, EMAS 2014, Paris, France, Revised Selected Papers 2, pp. 351–366. Springer International Publishing (2014)
10. Fuller, A., Fan, Z., Day, C., Barlow, C.: Digital twin: enabling technologies, challenges and open research. IEEE Access 8, 108952–108971 (2020)
11. Girardi, R., Leite, A.: A knowledge-based tool for multi-agent domain engineering. Knowl. Based Syst. 21(7), 604–611 (2008)
12. Herd, B., Miles, S., McBurney, P., Luck, M.: Verification and validation of agent-based simulations using approximate model checking. In: Alam, S.J., Parunak, H.V.D. (eds.) Multi-Agent-Based Simulation XIV, pp. 53–70. Springer, Berlin Heidelberg, Berlin, Heidelberg (2014)
13. Hogan, A., et al.: Knowledge graphs. ACM Comput. Surv. (Csur) 54(4), 1–37 (2021)
14. Kehoe, J.: Creating reproducible agent based models using formal methods. In: Multi-Agent Based Simulation XVII: International Workshop, MABS 2016, Singapore, Singapore, May 10, 2016, Revised Selected Papers 17, pp. 42–70. Springer (2017)
15. Mascardi, V., Ancona, D., Barbieri, M., Bordini, R.H., Ricci, A.: Cool-agentspeak: endowing agentspeak-dl agents with plan exchange and ontology services. Web Intell. Agent Syst. Int. J. 12(1), 83–107 (2014)

16. Mathieu, P., Routier, J.C., Secq, Y.: Towards a pragmatic use of ontologies in multi-agent platforms. In: Palade, V., Howlett, R.J., Jain, L. (eds.) International Conference on Knowledge-Based Intelligent Information & Engineering Systems, pp. 1395–1402. Springer, Berlin Heidelberg, Berlin, Heidelberg (2003)

17. Nishimura, Y., Shimura, T., Izumi, K., Yoshihara, K.: Design and evaluations of multi-agent simulation model for electric power sharing among households. In: Swarup, S., Savarimuthu, B.T.R. (eds.) Multi-Agent-Based Simulation XXI, pp. 41–53. Springer International Publishing, Cham (2021)

18. Parsons, B., Vidal, J.M., Huynh, N., Snyder, R.: Automatic generation of agent behavior models from raw observational data. In: Grimaldo, F., Norling, E. (eds.) Multi-Agent-Based Simulation XV, pp. 121–132. Springer International Publishing, Cham (2015)

19. Poveda, G., Schumann, R.: An ontology-driven approach for modeling a multi-agent-based electricity market. In: Multiagent System Technologies: 14th German Conference, MATES 2016, Klagenfurt, Österreich, September 27–30, 2016. Proceedings 14, pp. 27–40. Springer (2016)

20. Ralitera, T., Payet, D., Aky, N., Courdier, R.: The temporality model time scheduling approach: a practical application. In: Davidsson, P., Verhagen, H. (eds.) Multi-Agent-Based Simulation XIX, pp. 115–125. Springer International Publishing, Cham (2019)

21. Santos, G., Pinto, T., Vale, Z.: Multi-agent systems society for power and energy systems simulation. In: Davidsson, P., Verhagen, H. (eds.) Multi-Agent-Based Simulation XIX, pp. 126–137. Springer International Publishing, Cham (2019)

22. Sheldon, F.T., Elmore, M., Potok, T.E.: An ontology-based software agent system case study. In: 2003 International Symposium on Information Technology (ITCC 2003), 28–30 April 2003, Las Vegas, NV, USA, pp. 500–506. IEEE Computer Society, Los Alamitos, CA, USA (2003)

23. Tran, Q.N., Low, G.: MOBMAS: a methodology for ontology-based multi-agent systems development. Inf. Softw. Technolol. 50(7–8), 697–722 (2008)

24. Trojahn, C., Quaresma, P., Vieira, R.: Conjunctive queries for ontology based agent communication in mas. In: 7th International Joint Conference on Autonomous Agents and Multiagent Systems (AAMAS 2008), Estoril, Portugal, May 12–16, 2008, vol. 2, pp. 829–836 (2008)

Inverse Generative Approach for Identifying Agent-Based Models from Stochastic Primitives

Gayani P.D.P. Senanayake$^{(\boxtimes)}$ and Minh Kieu

Department of Civil and Environmental Engineering, University of Auckland,
Auckland 1010, New Zealand
gsen299@aucklanduni.ac.nz
http://www.cee.auckland.ac.nz/

Abstract. Genetic Programming (GP) evolves computer programs to solve problems while showing promising avenues for discovering complex behavioural rules in agent-based models (ABMs). Since existing efforts to learn ABM structures in the field of Inverse Generative Social Science (IGSS) have concentrated on combining domain-specific primitives for deterministic rule generation, this paper evolves interpretable agent logic from scratch comprised of stochastic primitives for decision tree nodes. We show the adaptability of our approach by applying it to discover models representing human behaviour targeting data generated from existing conceptual models. Our findings demonstrate that IGSS successfully identified the reference model's stochastic behaviour, with six of the top ten evolved rules matching the age-based random exit selection strategy. However, permutation importance analysis revealed that distance-based exit selection and gender similarity metrics demonstrated higher significance than age-based parameters, despite the latter being fundamental to the reference model. This apparent discordance can be attributed to the stochastic initialisation of agent attributes within the ABM simulation environment. While consistent convergence was observed by the fifth generation, the presence of substantial fitness fluctuations highlighted inherent challenges in learning from noisy data. This emerges as a critical challenge in stochastic ABM model discovery, necessitating the development of novel methodologies to guide the evolution of tree-based rules in genetic algorithms that are robust against noise-induced variations.

Keywords: Inverse Modelling · Genetic Programming · Agent-Based Modelling · Pedestrian Behaviour

1   Introduction

In the field of agent-based simulations and generative social science, it is crucial to specify all possible intra-agent equations in order to create accurate models of social systems. Those models can replicate actual dynamics to provide causal

© The Author(s), under exclusive license to Springer Nature Switzerland AG 2025
J. Thompson and I. Stankov (Eds.): MABS 2024, LNAI 15583, pp. 70–86, 2025.
https://doi.org/10.1007/978-3-031-88017-9_6

inference. This requires a careful understanding of human behavioural dynamics and decision-making processes. Agent-based models (ABMs) take a bottom-up approach for modelling systems, with macro-level behaviours emerging from the interactions of agents operating at the micro-level. While ABMs are capable of capturing the heterogeneity of human behaviour and providing in-depth analysis of agent interactions, the decisions made by individual agents are often guided by a predefined set of rules [1,36]. The formulation of these rules for individual behaviours typically requires manual effort by the modeller, which can be time-consuming and heavily dependent on the domain expertise and assumptions. This leads to modeller bias and loss of simulation realism and reduces the possibility of investigating actual trends [8,19].

To address this limitation, several approaches, including modelling protocols known as pattern-oriented modelling (POM) and Machine Learning (ML) based simulation methodologies have been proposed. POM is a technique that involves testing patterns of different theories by manually creating multiple candidate models to match a real-world scenario, which can introduce several possible behavioural foundations for the same observed explanandum while also introduce implementation risks and inconsistencies across models [11,35]. Beyond simulating potential macro-level behaviours of complex systems, ABMs offer the ability to work backwards with ML from real-world data, determining lower-level agent rules that reconstruct higher-level observed dynamics [12]. ML, on the other hand, is a data-driven approach that can enable the reverse implementation of ABM. It uses algorithms to discover patterns and make predictions based on past experiences. Many ML techniques act as black boxes, such as artificial neural networks, support vector machines, and random forests. Although they are powerful for predictions, these opaque models do not elucidate the decision processes or causal mechanisms that produce their outputs [26,39]. They are mainly focused on predictive accuracy rather than interpretation of results. In recent years, a promising evolutionary approach to addressing this challenge has been the use of Genetic Programming (GP) in agent-based simulations. GP, a subset of ML, provides a method for automatically discovering and evolving the rules or mechanisms that govern individual agent behaviour in an ABM [27,37]. This concept of generating rules rather than deductively testing theories to work backwards from data to underlying data-generating processes in an inductive manner while building explanations from the bottom up is called Inverse Generative Social Science (IGSS).

This emerging field of IGSS offers a novel approach to model discovery by generating potential explanatory ABMs for a target phenomenon, as opposed to modelling a singular pattern for micro-behavioural behaviour and testing its validity as is done in generative social science models [12]. This approach entails treating agent architecture as an output of the model rather than an input, and utilising ML algorithms to discern the rules or equations governing agent behaviour [32]. However, existing IGSS papers have also focused primarily on evolving deterministic agent rules and models keeping deterministic nodes in the decision tree [12,13,29,32]. This paper aims to explore the search space of decision trees in IGSS with stochastic nodes. This facilitates the development of highly stochastic ABMs properly capturing behavioural stochasticity, for instance, pedestrian behaviour and movements are inherently stochastic. This is supported by using the case study of pedestrian behaviour of people leaving the train station. We hypothesise that stochastic IGSS can be a more data-driven and systematic way to develop stochastic ABMs, rather than solely relying on predefined rules and modeller assumptions.

In Sect. 2, background information on the research area and case study model is introduced with sufficient detail for the subsequent manipulation of its structure to be understood. Then, in Sect. 3, an overall process of model discovery is introduced, with a particular focus on the evolutionary computing tools used to search through the space of model structures. Results of the model discovery process for the case study are provided in Sect. 4. Finally, the findings are discussed in detail in Sect. 5 with future directions for research on this exciting topic.

2   Background

2.1   Related Work

The generative social sciences paradigm argues that explaining macro-scale societal patterns requires modelling the micro-level mechanisms by which they arise from individual interactions [5]. ABM is axiomatic to this approach [2,38]. Such models integrate pedestrian navigation at the individual level by specifying simple movement rules, allowing complex system-level dynamics such as collision, exit selection, and congestion to emerge [17]. Most pedestrian ABMs rely on hand-crafted deterministic or probabilistic rules dictating acceleration, direction changes, collision avoidance, route choices, etc. [25]. A significant advances have been made in pedestrian modelling, while exploring the integration of stochastic elements into these agent-based behavioural decision-making systems. Early studies demonstrated adding stochastic components for navigation decisions or wait times at bottlenecks/intersections as it can improve model realism [24]. Recent empirical findings on crowd disasters highlight complex cognitive and social dynamics such as stochastic panic behaviours and peer influence effects [28,33]. However, most prevailing models take narrow approaches, modifying one or two isolated rules rather than searching search space for all possible stochastic pedestrian mechanisms [22]. This generally lacks an empirical grounding for their stipulated behavioural mechanisms [23].

Recently, the vision for "Inverse Generative Social Science" (IGSS) has been articulated, applying evolutionary computation to automate the discovery of generative ABMs. IGSS employs ML and other computational techniques to uncover the underlying mechanisms that give rise to social phenomena [7]. Methodologies ranging from GP to classifiers leverage Darwinian selection to evolve free-form equations, simulations, or programs according to fitness objectives [18,34]. Existing IGSS research demonstrations have focused on matching observable patterns in residential segregation, alcohol consumption, flocking dynamics and other domains. [12–15] proposed a promising framework for IGSS; Evolutionary Model Discovery (EMD), the first novel methodology for IGSS research. It automates the discovery of explanatory individual-level mechanisms behind emergent social phenomena using GP. They evolved agent decision rules to generate mixed patterns of residential segregation and integration behaviours. Rules were represented as mathematical equations combining hypothesised causal factors such as racial bias and isolation. A genetic program optimised combinations of these factors over generations to maximise the fitness metric indicating mixed patterns. [21] applied EMD to automate rule discovery irrigation cooperation dilemmas. The EMD methodology was further developed by [29–32] by the application of multi-objective evolutionary computation for IGSS. Using multi-objective grammar-based genetic programming (MOGGP), they treat social science theories as modular components that are combined in different arrangements to match historical targets on alcohol consumption trends. Trade-offs emerge between model fit, complexity, and theoretical coherence. Their approach searches over and tests alternative formulations of theories like social norms and social roles, promoting theoretical diversity. Model structures balance explanatory power against interpretability, with the goal of generating empirically grounded mechanistic explanations that can inform policy. [9] demonstrated an approach to automatically learn interpretable symbolic agent-based models from basic mathematical building blocks using GP. Without relying on domain knowledge, they evolve agent update rules as mathematical/logical functions that accurately replicate target flocking and opinion dynamics patterns.

Prior notable works in IGSS have focused mainly on evolving deterministic decision rules, whether domain-specific [14] or based on basic operators [9,30]. [21] introduced inherent stochasticity by evolving rules with random factor (terminal comparator). This paper introduces both deterministic and stochastic rules by introducing a random comparator node other than argmax and argmin nodes to the search space. Agents choose between behavioural exits deterministically or stochastically based on a probability calculated from distance, crowd and other factors. While these factors combine deterministically, final exit selection incorporates randomness - probabilistically picking min, max, or random exit. This explores whether uncertainty in strategy selection, rather than strategy execution, better explains human decisions. Stochasticity is critical for accurately representing the variability inherent to pedestrian behaviours. The emergent vision for IGSS offers newfound promise to automate the discovery of stochastic generative models across social science domains. However, pioneering applications have only begun targeting simpler deterministic search spaces. This paper's proposed case study, applying IGSS techniques to induce fully stochastic pedestrian movement from pseudo-truth data, will help advance the state-of-the-art. The expected contributions are manifold: substantiating the feasibility of automated stochastic model induction, enhancing the empirical validity of generative pedestrian simulations, and revealing novel behavioural insights to better design built environments.

2.2   Agent-Based Model: Station-Sim

To demonstrate IGSS concept with stochasticity, a simplified ABM of pedestrian behaviour, StationSim was employed, depicting generic human crowd flow. The StationSim model aims to capture key factors influencing pedestrian movement and congestion in train stations. The station layout is abstracted as a 2D grid with configurable entrances, exits, and sample agent trajectories exhibiting movement and interaction dynamics as shown in the Fig. 1.

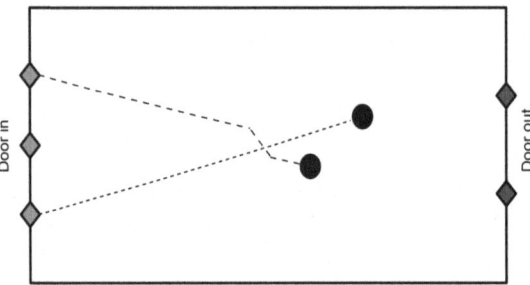

Fig. 1. The StationSim environment with 3 entrances and 2 exit doors.

In StationSim, agents emulate passengers exiting a train and crossing a station platform to leave through one of several exits. The key entities in the model are the agents, representing individual pedestrians with attributes such as location, speed, and movement history, and the station layout with configurable dimensions, entrances, and exits. At model initialisation, N agents are instantiated and enter the rectangular platform environment at a steady rate via one of three randomly assigned entrance points. Following that, they are assigned desired exit gate location randomly at the entrance. Each agent is navigated across the platform given a maximum intended speed sampled from a Gaussian distribution, which is a common assumption in pedestrian modeling literature [4] and it simplifies the heterogeneity of real-world pedestrian populations. During navigation, faster agents encounter slower agents obstructing their paths, triggering avoidance behaviours. When such interactions occur, the impeded agent randomly selects either a left or right manoeuvre to circumvent the slower agent. This stochastic local collision response induces emergent macro-level congestion patterns that vary across model executions. The simulation concludes when all agents have entered the platform environment and successfully exited.

The model's conceptual framework is based on established theories in social science field, such as the social force model [16] and the principle of least effort [40]. For example, the agent's navigation towards their desired exit while avoiding collisions is inspired by the social force model, which postulates that pedestrians are influenced by attractive forces towards their goals and repulsive forces from other individuals and barriers. Moreover, the model incorporates stochastic elements to represent the inherent variability in human behavior, such as random fluctuations in walking speed and direction. The model assumes a steady inflow of agents, homogeneous decision-making rules, and perfect knowledge of the station layout. While the model simplifies certain aspects of reality, such as group dynamics, queueing behavior, and multi-level structures, it captures the essential elements of pedestrian movement and interactions in a station setting. The three most important characteristics of this model are a) individual heterogeneity: each agent has a desired maximum speed, b) agent interactions: agents are not allowed to occupy the same space and try to overtake the slower agent, and c) emergence: crowding is an emergent property of the system that arises as a result of the choice of exit and their maximum speed [3,20]. By explicitly stating these assumptions and limitations, the StationSim model provides a clear conceptual framework for understanding and interpreting the simulation results in the context of pedestrian behavioural Modelling.

3   Methodology

ABMs capture emergent social processes but may get complex. Evolutionary algorithms provide a robust optimization framework for systematically exploring ABM structures and parameter spaces. Integrating them brings together individual and evolutionary dynamics for more plausible yet interpretable models [10]. The IGSS approach involves the following steps as described by [7]. First, stipulating a macroscopic target pattern observed empirically or from theoretical models that one seeks to generate from the bottom-up (Step 1). For example, patterns of residential segregation, trends in alcohol consumption, flocking movements, etc. Rather than hand-design full agent rules, one then specifies more basic behavioural rule primitives and permissible ways of combining them (Steps 2 and 3). This includes factors like racial preferences, social conformity, collision avoidance and logical operators like if-then conditions, mathematical operations, nesting/recursion limits, etc. A fitness metric is chosen to compute model-target alignment, such as error distances (Step 4), and an evolutionary algorithm, such as GP and grammatical evolution, is selected to search the space of rule combinations (Step 5). Evolution proceeds according to this metric until reaching preset limits (Step 6). The end result is one or more ABMs with evolved interaction rules that can successfully replicate the phenotype target pattern.

In lieu of real-world data, we utilise output from the StationSim simulation as target data for testing our approach. This allows us to validate the capability of our method to automatically reverse-engineer agent logic recapitulating provided reference data patterns. The evolved decision trees are automatically translated into modular Python code to initialise and run the evolved models for fitness evaluation.

3.1   Hypothesised Alternate Factors Influencing Exit Selection Decision

The agents in the original StationSim model select the exits randomly at the entrance gate. First, the StationSim model of the static exit selection rule was refined into a dynamic rule evaluated per time step. So, the IGSS is applied to the changed model rule where agent select the exit randomly at each time step. Then, the set of hypothesized factors that could influence an agent's exit choice, such as distance, crowd density were defined to be implemented as primitives in the GP framework. To expand the realism of simulated human decision-making, we draw on the Agent_Zero framework proposed by [6], incorporating rational, social, and emotional dimensions into exit choice calculations. As shown in Table 1 the provided hypothesised factors are terminal nodes for the decision tree rules. We introduce each factor as a function(probability between [0,1]): compare_distance (F_d), compare_neighbouring_crowd (F_c), compare_age (F_a), and compare_gender (F_g). The categorisation of decision factors into categories provides a conceptual framework, though the mapping of specific variables can be subjective. The "rational" factor is represented by the comparison of distances to exits, reflecting the assumption that pedestrians tend to choose the nearest exitand the "emotional" and "social" factors are captured by the agents' tendency to follow the crowd or align with the behavior of similar individuals in terms of age and gender.

Table 1. Primitive set used for exit selection of StationSim model

Node	Syntax	Return Type
MinOf	min-one-of (exits)[comparator]	exit
MaxOf	max-one-of (exits)[comparator]	exit
RandomOf	random-one-of (exits)[comparator]	exit
+	comparator + comparator	comparator
-	comparator - comparator	comparator
Potentialexits	exit-x exit-y	exits
Rational factors		
CompareDistance	((distance x-of-exit y-of-exit) / totDistance)	comparator
Emotional / Social factors		
CompareCrowd	((sum [num-agents] in-radius of 5) / totCrowd)	comparator
CompareAge	((((1-(Agent [age] - mean [age] of agents)) / maxAge) / totRelativeAge)	comparator
CompareGender	((sum [num-agents] with same (gender) of agent) / totAgents)	comparator

Next, the pseudo-truth dataset by running the StationSim model with a predefined exit selection rule was created to be used as the target dataset. The pseudo-truth StationSim model as mentioned in the Table 3 used to collect the target data utilised for the experiment. In this stochastic rule (later mentioned in the paper as "pseudo-truth rule"), each agent randomly selects an exit, but the probability distribution is weighted based on the similarity of the agent's age compared to the average age of agents near the exits. We then used the

Deap Library to set up the GP experiment. This library parsed the StationSim model and generated a set of rules based on the provided factors. To ensure the evolution of valid agent logic, the GP components enforce strong typing between terminals nodes and the comparator nodes. As shown in Table 1, each proposed factor has an associated type definition. Comparator nodes embed code for assessing exit options on normalised sensor inputs, enabling fair mathematical operations across different factor types within the decision trees. Later they were compared by the MinOf, MaxOf, and randomOf nodes to exactly select what exit the agent selects based on exit options. By designing GP building blocks to align with programming syntax requirements, the system constrains exploration to the space of compilable agent behaviours. Legal code generation facilitates the translation of the evolved trees into executable agent-based model implementations.

For example, a combination of factors R(x) may be;

$$R(x) = F_d + F_c - F_a \tag{1}$$

Agents then decide the exit to select, e', using argmax, argmin, and random over the possible exits defined and considering the final probability based on R(x) value:

$$e' = argminR(x) \tag{2}$$

The GP algorithm evolved a population of candidate exit selection rules, represented as syntax trees, over multiple generations. Each candidate rule was evaluated by injecting it into the StationSim model, running simulations, and comparing the resulting exit distributions to the pseudo-truth data using a fitness function. The evolutionary process employed tournament selection, crossover, and mutation operators to create new generations of candidate rules. By representing decision rules as modular, reusable factor functions, the factor composition can be systematically mutated towards higher simulation fitness against macro-level data patterns. Finally, we analysed the evolved rules and their fitness scores to identify the most promising exit selection strategies and assess the importance of different factors in reproducing the target patterns. Table 3 lists the most fitted "candidate rules" for the pseudo-truth rule.

For model simplicity, we assume agents have full information on all exit sites. The goal is to minimising divergence between simulated and target data on agent counts who selected each exit over time. Specifically, Eq. 3 defines model error as the sum over all time steps t of the squared differences between the simulated (Y) and actual agent (Y') counts exiting through each exit (e) at each time step (i). Individual GP tree fitness scores report aggregate error across a 1000-time step StationSim model evaluation. By explicitly fitting agent logic to match exit distributions, the system evolves behaviours governing exit choice to reconstruct emergent system-level patterns exhibited in the reference data.

$$Loss = \sum_{i=1}^{t} (Y_{i,e} - Y'_{i,e})^2 \tag{3}$$

4 Results

We executed three independent GP runs to evolve the StationSim agent exit selection logic. The configuration applied 20 generations with a population of 10 tree individuals, using crossover and mutation to explore the space of possible decision rules. Each candidate tree was translated into a complete StationSim implementation and simulated for 1000 steps. The aggregate deviation between the agent exit distributions and reference outputs determined error. We set key evolutionary parameters as 0.8 crossover rate, 0.2 mutation rate, minimum tree depth of 2, and maximum depth of 10. The minimum depth allows the first layer to be a random, minimum, or maximum function, with the second layer introducing a single factor influencing choice. Through iterative evaluation and refinement of agent behaviour trees, the system converges on rule sets replicating emergent circulation patterns from the original model.

Table 2 lists the top 10 evolved decision trees with corresponding error scores, ranked by similarity to the reference data. As expected, most appearing rule in the result is to select the exit gate randomly based on similarity by age. Figure 2 displays the mean and standard deviation of aggregate loss value of each generation decreasing over generations as agent behaviours improve. This close match confirms the capability to accurately reverse engineer the key exit choice logic governing circulation dynamics in the original StationSim model. The full GP experiment required approximately 20 h of computation time.

Table 2. The 10 top candidate models.

Run	Gen	Rule	Agg: Error
0	15	Exit = Randomly based on the similarity by age	4446.27
0	4	Exit = Randomly based on the similarity by age	4713.41
2	17	Exit = Minimum based on the combination of difference between (similarity by gender and crowdness) and combination of (distance and similarity by age)	4839.07
2	13	Exit = Minimum based on the distance	4926.21
0	3	Exit = Randomly based on the similarity by age	4960.11
0	10	Exit = Randomly based on the similarity by age	4967.73
0	19	Exit = Minimum based on the distance	5001.91
2	5	Exit = Randomly based on the similarity by age	5009.29
0	18	Exit = Randomly based on the similarity by age	5029.51

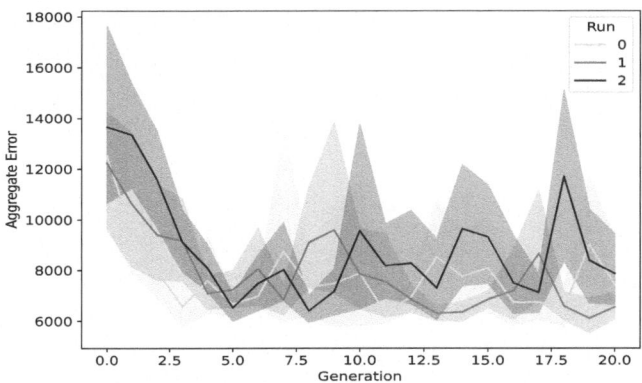

Fig. 2. Mean Aggregate Error over Generations

Figure 3 displays the Aggregate error of the best agent logic discovered in each GP run over generations. Convergence to low error solutions appears gradual, likely due to the limited generations and pseudo-truth data set based on a stochastic rule. Figure 4 plots the size of the optimum trees found so far per generation in each run, indicating one run maintains compact decision rules while the others evolve between maximum allowed depth mostly in early generations. Between runs, variability in tree shape and speed of fitness improvement by lowering the error highlights the stochastic nature of GP optimisation. Additional computational budget for longer runs and larger populations could improve solution quality and convergence rates.

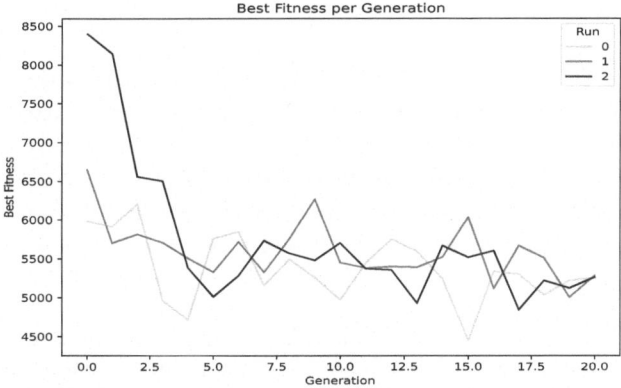

Fig. 3. The best model by generation in each GP runs

For easy Visualisation in later plot, the unique candidate rules in the Table 2 are shortlisted in the Table 3 where pseudo-truth rule and the candidate Rule 1 are the same.

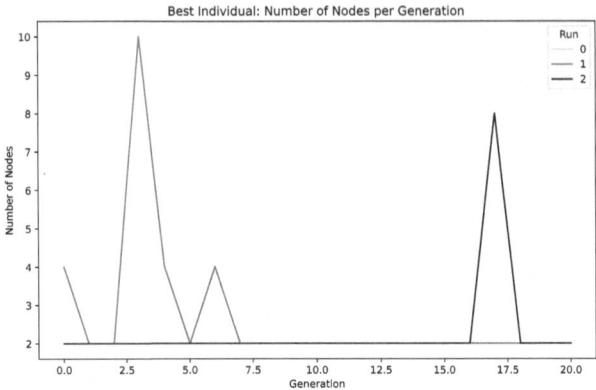

Fig. 4. Size of the best individuals

Table 3. The unique top three candidate rules.

Model	Exit Selection Rule
rule for generating target data	
Pseudo-truth	Exit = Randomly based on the similarity by age
candidate rules	
Rule 1	Exit = Randomly based on the similarity by age
Rule 3	Exit = Minimum based on the combination of difference between (similarity by gender and crowdness) and combination of (distance and similarity by age)
Rule 4	Exit = Minimum based on the distance

Figure 5 and Table 4 exhibit simulation results from three top evolved decision rules (rules 1, 3, and 4 in the Table 3) compared against each other across 100 simulation runs. These rules were selected based on their performance in reproducing the patterns observed in the pseudo-truth dataset, which was generated using Rule 1. In this analysis, Rule 1 serves as the benchmark, representing the "ground truth" or the target behavior we aim to replicate. The other evolved rules (Rules 3 and 4) are evaluated based on how closely they match the performance of Rule 1.

When compared to Rule 1, Rule 2 has a similar median aggregate error score. Interestingly, the Rule 2 spread is fully contained within the Rule 1 distribution, indicating greater consistency. This shows Rule 2 can almost replicate Rule 1's performance, serving as a plausible explanatory model even if falling short of ground truth decisions. Conversely, Rule 3's mean is considerably lower at 7710.24, with a higher deviation of 1579.33. So it fails to approach Rule 1 aggregate outcomes while retaining a similar variability profile. Concretely, Rule 2 approximates truth better statistically, while Rule 3 diverges on overall accuracy but emulates variance characteristics. Given these data details, Rule 2 provides a feasible decision theory not far from ground truth, whereas Rule 3 does not explain the core patterns well despite matching uncertainty levels.

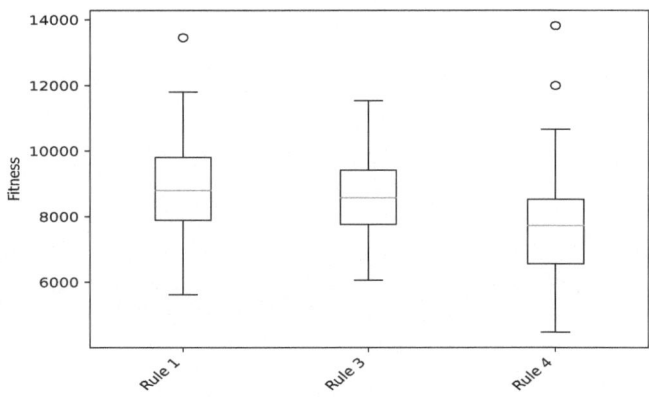

Fig. 5. Comparisons of 100 samples of three of the top-performing models

Table 4. Mean and Standard Deviation (SD) of best models.

Rule	Mean	SD
Exit = Randomly based on the similarity by age	8843.97	1422.62
Exit = Minimum based on the combination of difference between (similarity by gender and crowdness) and combination of (distance and similarity by age)	8595.48	1208.07
Exit = Minimum based on the distance	7710.23	1579.32

Factor importance obtained through permutation accuracy importance techniques can be seen in Fig. 6. It is calculated by randomly shuffling the presence values of each factor in isolation and quantifying the resulting decrease in error prediction performance of the trained random forest model. The result indicated compare_distance as the most influential contributor to model fitness (error reduction), with Similarity_by_gender also showing a stronger role in exit choice behaviour than the other hypothesised factors.

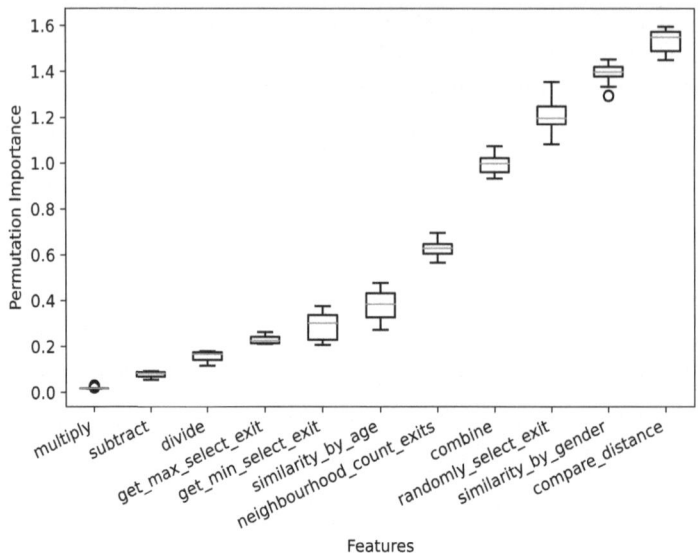

Fig. 6. Feature Importance Analysis

5 Discussion

Our study goes beyond a mere demonstration of a specific parameter setup and simulation execution. By employing the Inverse Generative Social Science (IGSS) approach with GP, we aim to shed light on the novel methodology to discover stochastic ABM models. The StationSim model serves as a flexible platform to explore the space of plausible behavioral rules and test hypotheses about the factors influencing that decision-making behaviour. The evolutionary process of rule discovery allows the modellers to uncover novel and emergent strategies that may not be readily apparent from traditional deductive approaches. The rules governing agents in current applications of IGSS thus far have been limited to deterministic specifications. Developing techniques to effectively search over stochastic mechanisms remains an open challenge for uncovering the full promise of generative modelling. Advancing stochastic IGSS methods suited to capturing the inherent randomness of human behaviour and social systems represents an important frontier.

In this study, we incorporated stochasticity in model discovery in several ways. Same as [21], stochastic factors (terminal node) were introduce that randomly assign values for the agent in ABM model initialisation and also stochastic comparator node (get_random) other than the get_max or get_min deterministic comparators. Comparator nodes responsible for selecting exits based on the probability calculated by factor combinations. The study utilised GP to evolve syntex tree rules where those rules were injected to Python-based ABM for fitness calculation against pseudo-truth data set. The result found that IGSS can pick up the model with the same stochastic rule used for collecting pseudo-truth data as the most fitted model.

There are additional insights to be had from the models generated and subsequent factor analysis. We note that rule 4, which is a diterministic factor based on the distance in Table 2 shows a lower medium and mean error value as illustrated in Fig. 5 and Table 4 when compared to rule 1, which is the benchmark to the specific pseudo-truth dataset considered in rule evolution. On the other hand, contrary to the reference model exit selection behaviour of the StationSim model, where an agent would randomly select the exits in relation to age, the permutation accuracy importance results show that agents are most likely to select exit randomly over min and max, but distance as the most important factor over similarity by age. This can be attributed to the stochastic initialisation of agent attributes within the ABM simulation environment. That leads the algorithm to learn from noise while showing inconsistent convergence after fifth generation. This highlights the necessity to guide the evolution of tree-based rules in genetic algorithms that are robust against noise-induced variations.

In this genetic algorithm experiment seeking to evolve stochastic rules, the randomness in Rule 1 could allow it to achieve high error scores against the pseudo-truth, but the deterministic rules seem to do better when evaluated across many repeated trials. Further, reliance on a single static pseudo-truth data mapping for fitness evaluation might have led to overfitting. Though Rule 1 scored best on fitness against that target data, Rules 3 and 4 may be more robust rules in general. There may be gene interactions happening in the genetic algorithm evolution process that lead to unexpected emergent behaviours. The evolved rules may exploit certain combinations and nonlinearities.

To promote the evolution of broadly generalisable stochastic rules, multiple mechanisms must be employed to overcome this training overfitting effect. Specifically, multiple mapping of simulated data with pseudo-truth data to calculate an average fitness score. Further the fitness metrics can be advanced to capture stochasticity like mean and sd considering all mappings for each candidate rule. k-fold cross-validation can be used based on the data availability so that rules are evaluated against multiple held-out data partitions rather than just a singular target output mapping. Additionally, explicit incentives such as bonus fitness rewards for error reduction should be incorporated for stochastic behaviours exhibited in promising rule candidates across evaluations. Other enhancements include expanding the rule search space, rule complexity vs interpretability and forcing rules to generalise across iteratively updated pseudo-truth data. By emphasizing rule generalisation beyond narrow accuracy gains on limited training distributions, the genetic algorithm can better identify robust and widely applicable stochastic rules for simulation modelling.

Currently, all the agent models being tested assume that everyone follows the same decision-making strategy. Allowing different agents to use different strategies could potentially improve heterogeneity in agent behaviour and might lead to models that fit the human data even better. Further, as [32] suggested exploring the whole model without just evolving one sub-model will uncover the true potential of IGSS. Future work could introduce agent heterogeneity and apply IGSS to learn personalised collision avoidance behaviours with the StationSim model.

This work adds to a growing body of literature [9,14,21,30] demonstrating the promise of IGSS for agent-based social science research. By automating the discovery of the micro-level rules able to recreate emergence, these methods can strengthen model accuracy, plausibility, and generalisability compared to purely theoretical specifications. As IGSS matures to handle richer data and more complex collective dynamics, it may provide fundamental new insights into causal mechanisms in social systems. However, care must be taken to avoid overfitting and ensure model interpretability. Overall, the study provides insights on new concept of IGSS that use GP for generation of generative models that could provide policy-relevant explanations over purely predictive functions.

Acknowledgments. This study was funded by Auckland Doctoral Scholarship by University of Auckland.

Disclosure of Interests. The authors have no competing interests to declare that are relevant to the content of this article.

References

1. Badham, J., Chattoe-Brown, E., Gilbert, N., Chalabi, Z., Kee, F., Hunter, R.F.: Developing agent-based models of complex health behaviour. Health Place **54**, 170–177 (2018)
2. Camillen, F., et al.: Multi agent simulation of pedestrian behavior in closed spatial environments. In: 2009 IEEE Toronto International Conference Science and Technology for Humanity (TIC-STH), pp. 375–380. IEEE (2009)
3. Clay, R., Kieu, L.M., Ward, J.A., Heppenstall, A., Malleson, N.: Towards real-time crowd simulation under uncertainty using an agent-based model and an unscented kalman filter. In: International Conference on Practical Applications of Agents and Multi-agent Systems, pp. 68–79. Springer (2020)
4. Daamen, W., Hoogendoorn, S.P.: Free speed distributions-based on empirical data in different traffic conditions. In: Pedestrian and Evacuation Dynamics 2005, pp. 13–25. Springer (2007)
5. Epstein, J.M.: Agent-based computational models and generative social science. Complexity **4**(5), 41–60 (1999)
6. Epstein, J.M.: Agent_Zero: Toward Neurocognitive Foundations for Generative Social Science. Princeton University Press (2014)
7. Epstein, J.M.: Inverse generative social science: Backward to the future. J. Artif. Soc. Soc. Simul. JASSS **26**(2) (2023)
8. Galpin, V., Zoń, N., Wilsdorf, P., Gilmore, S.: Mesoscopic modelling of pedestrian movement using Carma and its tools. ACM Trans. Model. Comput. Simul. (TOMACS) **28**(2), 1–26 (2018)
9. Greig, R., Major, C., Pacholska, M., Bending, S., Arranz, J.: Learning interpretable logic for agent-based models from domain independent primitives. J. Artif. Soc. Soc. Simul. **26**(2) (2023)

10. Grifoni, P., D'Ulizia, A., Ferri, F.: Computational methods and grammars in language evolution: a survey. Artif. Intell. Rev. **45**, 369–403 (2016)
11. Grimm, V., et al.: Pattern-oriented modeling of agent-based complex systems: lessons from ecology. Science **310**(5750), 987–991 (2005)
12. Gunaratne, C., Garibay, I.: Alternate social theory discovery using genetic programming: towards better understanding the artificial anasazi. In: Proceedings of the Genetic and Evolutionary Computation Conference, pp. 115–122 (2017)
13. Gunaratne, C., Garibay, I.: Evolutionary model discovery of causal factors behind the socio-agricultural behavior of the ancestral pueblo. PLoS ONE **15**(12), e0239922 (2020)
14. Gunaratne, C., Hatna, E., Epstein, J.M., Garibay, I.: Generating mixed patterns of residential segregation: an evolutionary approach. J. Artif. Soc. Soc. Simul. **26**(2) (2023)
15. Gunaratne, C., Rand, W., Garibay, I.: Inferring mechanisms of response prioritization on social media under information overload. Sci. Rep. **11**(1), 1346 (2021)
16. Helbing, D., Molnar, P.: Social force model for pedestrian dynamics. Phys. Rev. E **51**(5), 4282 (1995)
17. Karamouzas, I., Heil, P., Van Beek, P., Overmars, M.H.: A predictive collision avoidance model for pedestrian simulation. In: Motion in Games: Second International Workshop, MIG 2009, Zeist, The Netherlands, November 21–24, 2009. Proceedings 2, pp. 41–52. Springer (2009)
18. Krawiec, K., Liskowski, P.: Automatic derivation of search objectives for test-based genetic programming. In: European Conference on Genetic Programming, pp. 53–65. Springer (2015)
19. Li, D., Zhong, J.: Dimensionally aware multi-objective genetic programming for automatic crowd behavior modeling. ACM Trans. Model. Comput. Simul. (TOMACS) **30**(3), 1–24 (2020)
20. Malleson, N., Minors, K., Kieu, L.M., Ward, J.A., West, A.A., Heppenstall, A.: Simulating crowds in real time with agent-based modelling and a particle filter. arXiv preprint arXiv:1909.09397 (2019)
21. Miranda, L., Garibay, O.O., Baggio, J.: Evolutionary model discovery of human behavioral factors driving decision-making in irrigation experiments. J. Artif. Soc. Soc. Simul. **26**(2) (2023)
22. Papadimitriou, E., Yannis, G., Golias, J.: A critical assessment of pedestrian behaviour models. Transport. Res. F: Traffic Psychol. Behav. **12**(3), 242–255 (2009)
23. Pitts, R.C.: Reconsidering the concept of behavioral mechanisms of drug action. J. Exp. Anal. Behav. **101**(3), 422–441 (2014)
24. Ramos-Moreno, C., Ruiz-Teran, A.M., Stafford, P.J.: Impact of stochastic representations of pedestrian actions on serviceability response. In: Proceedings of the Institution of Civil Engineers-Bridge Engineering, vol. 174, pp. 113–128. Thomas Telford Ltd. (2021)
25. Schratter, M., Bouton, M., Kochenderfer, M.J., Watzenig, D.: Pedestrian collision avoidance system for scenarios with occlusions. In: 2019 IEEE Intelligent Vehicles Symposium (IV), pp. 1054–1060. IEEE (2019)
26. Sharma, S., Ogunlana, K., Scribner, D., Grynovicki, J.: Modeling human behavior during emergency evacuation using intelligent agents: a multi-agent simulation approach. Inf. Syst. Front. **20**, 741–757 (2018)
27. Smith, V.A.: Evolving an agent-based model to probe behavioral rules in flocks of cowbirds. In: ALIFE, vol. 2008, pp. 561–568 (2008)
28. Vizzari, G., Crociani, L., Bandini, S.: An agent-based model for plausible wayfinding in pedestrian simulation. Eng. Appl. Artif. Intell. **87**, 103241 (2020)

29. Vu, T.M., et al.: Multiobjective genetic programming can improve the explanatory capabilities of mechanism-based models of social systems. Complexity **2020**(1), 8923197 (2020)
30. Vu, T.M., Buckley, C., Duro, J.A., Brennan, A., Epstein, J.M., Purshouse, R.C.: Can social norms explain long-term trends in alcohol use? insights from inverse generative social science. J. Artif. Soc. Soc. Simul. JASSS **26**(2) (2023)
31. Vu, T.M., Davies, E., Buckley, C., Brennan, A., Purshouse, R.C.: Using multi-objective grammar-based genetic programming to integrate multiple social theories in agent-based modeling. In: Evolutionary Multi-Criterion Optimization: 11th International Conference, EMO 2021, Shenzhen, China, March 28–31, 2021, Proceedings 11, pp. 721–733. Springer (2021)
32. Vu, T.M., Probst, C., Epstein, J.M., Brennan, A., Strong, M., Purshouse, R.C.: Toward inverse generative social science using multi-objective genetic programming. In: Proceedings of the Genetic and Evolutionary Computation Conference, pp. 1356–1363 (2019)
33. Wang, J., Chen, M., Yan, W., Zhi, Y., Wang, Z.: A utility threshold model of herding-panic behavior in evacuation under emergencies based on complex network theory. SIMULATION **93**(2), 123–133 (2017)
34. Wehrens, R., Buydens, L.M.: Evolutionary optimisation: a tutorial. TrAC, Trends Anal. Chem. **17**(4), 193–203 (1998)
35. Wilensky, U., Rand, W.: Making models match: replicating an agent-based model. J. Artif. Soc. Soc. Simul. **10**(4), 2 (2007)
36. Zhang, B., Chan, W., Ukkusuri, S.V.: On the modelling of transportation evacuation: an agent-based discrete-event hybrid-space approach. J. Simul. **8**(4), 259–270 (2014)
37. Zhong, J., Luo, L., Cai, W., Lees, M.: Automatic rule identification for agent-based crowd models through gene expression programming. In: Proceedings of the 2014 International Conference on Autonomous Agents and Multi-agent Systems, pp. 1125–1132 (2014)
38. Zhou, Y.: Agent-based modeling and simulation for pedestrian movement behaviors in space: a review of applications and GIS issues. In: Geoinformatics 2008 and Joint Conference on GIS and Built Environment: Geo-Simulation and Virtual GIS Environments, vol. 7143, pp. 508–516. SPIE (2008)
39. Zhu, R., Becerik-Gerber, B., Lin, J., Li, N.: Behavioral, data-driven, agent-based evacuation simulation for building safety design using machine learning and discrete choice models. Adv. Eng. Inform. **55**, 101827 (2023)
40. Zipf, G.K.: The Principle of Least Effort. CH3 (1949)

Inferring Pedestrian Decision-Making Through Inverse Reinforcement Learning

Xiangmin Yang[1](✉)(iD), Liu Yang[2](✉)(iD), Arnab Majumdar[1](iD),
and Washington Ochieng[1](iD)

[1] Department of Civil and Environmental Engineering, Imperial College London,
London SW7 2AZ, UK
xiangmin.yang18@imperial.ac.uk
[2] School of Architecture, Southeast University, Nanjing 210096, China
yangliu2020@seu.edu.cn

Abstract. To effectively simulate crowd behavior, understanding the decision-making processes of pedestrians is paramount. This paper proposes a novel method for deducing pedestrians' decision-making by conceptualizing the sum of their reward function along the trajectory as a utility function. While inverse reinforcement learning has been successfully used to retrieve the reward function of pedestrians, the outcome of advanced training algorithms is in the format of neural networks. Due to the black-box nature of neural networks, model interpretability methods are utilized to extract attributions of each input feature. This paper introduces a coupled method of inverse reinforcement learning and model interpretability to infer pedestrians' decision-making on urban sidewalks based on the trajectory data collected in previous experiments. Furthermore, a preliminary test in a classical reinforcement learning environment cart pole is included to demonstrate the viability of the proposed method.

Keywords: Pedestrian decision-making · Pedestrian behavior simulation · Inverse reinforcement learning · Urban street

1 Introduction

Simulating crowd behavior through analytical models or simulation tools has proved its worth in the design of public spaces and planning for large gatherings [15]. Most advanced approaches for modelling multi-agent interactions within a crowd include direct trajectory prediction methods such as deep learning algorithms [23,26], as well as deriving the movement preference of a crowd through reinforcement learning [9,32].

Furthermore, a good practical performance of reinforcement learning greatly depends on the design of the reward function [13], which can be thought of as ranking various behaviors [8] as a response to environmental attributes, i.e., a decision-making process [1,38]. Consequently, a comprehensive understanding of

© The Author(s), under exclusive license to Springer Nature Switzerland AG 2025
J. Thompson and I. Stankov (Eds.): MABS 2024, LNAI 15583, pp. 87–97, 2025.
https://doi.org/10.1007/978-3-031-88017-9_7

decision-making is vital, and this can also facilitate the provision of a more comfortable walking environment [38] and assist in developing efficient crowd management strategies [17].

While applying reinforcement learning in practice, designing a reward function that is capable of encouraging socially acceptable behavior remains a significant challenge [13]. Inverse reinforcement learning (IRL), in contrast, is capable of deducing such reward functions by learning from the input data. Since the outcome of adversarial IRL is in the form of a neural network, interpretation methods are still needed to quantitatively assess the contribution of each environmental attribute on decision-making. Moreover, the explained reward function allows urban researchers to understand the mechanism between built environment design and pedestrian behavior, which, in turn, can improve the design of public spaces and provide a reference for agent modelling in similar scenarios.

Therefore, this paper aims to: (1) propose a framework for inferring pedestrians' decision-making in urban sidewalks, and (2) validate the usage of model interpretability in evaluating attributions of each input for the reward function neural network retrieved through IRL.

2   Literature Review

2.1   Pedestrian Decision-Making

The mechanism of decision-making for pedestrians, as identified by [38], involves a process of making trade-offs between desirable and undesirable attributes in the surrounding environments. Such a process is known as utility theory, which assumes that pedestrians assign a quantitative value (utility) to each attribute X_n. The utilities reflect the degree to which the corresponding attributes contribute to the actions made and are combined in a way commonly known as a utility function G_n. Under utility theory, each action pedestrians make could be viewed as an outcome of optimizing the utility function, as it stands for the mechanism of decision-making.

$$G_n = \beta_1 X_{n_1} + \beta_2 X_{n_2} + \cdots + \beta_k X_{n_k}.$$

Two approaches have been adopted widely to infer the relative utility for different attributes encountered during movement: scores given by participants using a questionnaire [6,31,40] and by means of a regression model based on experimental data [16,24,36]. However, both approaches suffer from drawbacks: pedestrians do not always perform in the way they declare in the questionnaire [30] and the regression model can only be used to decide the contribution of each factor toward action choice at a single timestep, often represented as discrete choices (e.g., choice of exit) [39].

In summary, a better approach for inferring the utility function for pedestrian decision-making is needed, one that can (1) quantify contributions of each attribute to pedestrians' movement preferences in real life and (2) comprehend movement preferences behind the entire trajectory.

As summarized by previous studies [21], common factors affecting pedestrian trajectory include movement direction, speed, and density of neighboring pedestrians. Additionally, built environment factors have also been identified as being associated with pedestrians' movement preferences [5]. For example, [10] highlighted that the design of street features, including sidewalk width, transparency of street walls, green spaces (including trees), and street furniture impacts pedestrians' movements.

2.2 Inverse Reinforcement Learning (IRL)

As an essential element of reinforcement learning, the reward function R can be used to infer an agent's intentions [13] and is often used to provide a reward signal during each transition along the trajectory. The sum of rewards along the trajectory τ could be viewed as a utility function [2]:

$$G(\tau) = \sum_{t=1}^{\tau} R_t,$$

while optimizing G, the optimal policy π^* is achieved, which stands for the preference of actions over the entire trajectory.

Inverse reinforcement learning [29], on the other hand, has been proposed to infer the reward function being optimized by expert agents. Such a method is considered necessary as it facilitates determining the relative weights of a multi-attribute reward function and constructs an intelligent agent capable of performing specific tasks akin to real-life experts.

In the field of pedestrian dynamics, IRL has been successful in: inferring a navigation policy for robots in human crowds [7,11,14], modeling interactions between pedestrians with vehicles [27,28] and cyclists [3], and predicting future trajectories [34]. This has exploited IRL's capacity for constructing intelligent agents but left the reward function itself unexplored.

Adversarial IRL [13,19] is a crucial framework proposed by [12] to infer a reward function based on generative adversarial networks. Such a method involves the training of a generator neural network G, together with a discriminator network D. The reward function can then be retrieved from D in the form of a neural network [13]. However, analyzing the reward function still poses challenges, as the neural network decision-making mechanism is not explicitly accessible [35].

In this research, we propose a new method to infer a pedestrian's decision-making process by combining inverse reinforcement learning and model interpretability. The result shall present the relative contribution of each attribute in the environment to pedestrian decisions, shedding light on the interplay between environment and pedestrians, and enabling more accurate multiagent modeling.

3   Methodology

3.1   Model Framework

Model Formation. The entire trajectory of pedestrians can be viewed as a Markov Decision Process (MDP) $M = (S, A, T, R, \gamma)$, where S is the state space; A is the action space; $T(s, s', a)$ is the transition probability from state s to s' under action a; R is the reward function; γ is the discount factor ranged on $[0, 1)$, indicating the level of preference for immediate reward over future reward.

As summarized above, common impact factors of pedestrian decision-making include pedestrian density, direction, and speed. From each pedestrian's perspective, the perceived information only includes the density and speeds of N pedestrians within their field of view h (often a 4 m, 180° sector [41]). The density is expressed in terms of the number of pedestrians within eyesight and categorized into two levels of speed: slow and fast, i.e.,

$$N_{\text{slow}} + N_{\text{fast}} = N_{\text{in sight}}.$$

This forms the foundation of agent state space S together with the current position X, speed V, and destination D_d. As this research focuses on urban sidewalk design, the width of the sidewalk W, the shortest distance to green space D_g, and the transparency of the street wall T (denoted by a binary number where 1 stands for transparent) are also combined to reflect the environmental impact. In summary, the state space S will be expressed as:

$$S = [\, X, \, V, \, D_d, \, h, \, N_{\text{slow}}, \, N_{\text{fast}}, \, W, \, D_g, \, T \,].$$

The action space A is denoted as:

$$A = [\, u, \, \omega \,],$$

where u stands for change of velocity, and ω is the change in direction.

Training Algorithm. Within the framework of Adversarial IRL, the generator G is the policy $\pi(a \mid s)$, which tries to generate occupancy measures similar to those in the expert demonstration.

The discriminator D, on the other side, aims to differentiate the generated state-action pair from expert demonstrations by minimizing the cross-entropy loss:

$$\log(1 - D(\tau)) - \log D(\tau)$$

Adversarial Inverse Reinforcement Learning (AIRL) proposed by [13] is utilized in this research due to its capability to recover a reward function that is robust to changes in environment dynamics. Compared with other adversarial IRL methods, such as GAIL [19], AIRL gives a special structure to the discriminator D:

$$D_{\theta,\varphi}(s, a, s') = \frac{\exp\{f_{\theta,\varphi}(s, a, s')\}}{\exp\{f_{\theta,\varphi}(s, a, s')\} + \pi(a \mid s)},$$

where $f_{\theta,\varphi}$, parametrized by θ and φ, is restricted to the learned reward network g_θ and a shaping term h_φ:

$$f_{\theta,\varphi}(s, a, s') = g_\theta(s, a) + \gamma\, h_\varphi(s') - h_\varphi(s).$$

Model Interpretability. Three model interpretability methods, namely feature ablation, Shapley value sampling (SVP), and Kernel SHAP, are explored in this research for their usage in explaining the reward function $g_\theta(s, a)$. All methods are aimed at evaluating the attribution of each input to the output of the neural network.

In feature ablation, each input is replaced with a baseline, and the attribution is calculated based on the impact of replacement on the output [33]. The concept of Shapley value is utilized in the other two methods, and it is based on concepts from cooperative game theory, in which all the input features collaborate together to accomplish one task (output). The attribution of each input feature is then calculated based on its impact on the output when it is added to permutations of other input features [37].

As it is computationally intensive to calculate all the permutations when the dimension of input features is large, alternatives have been proposed: SVP uses random sampling of permutations, and Kernel SHAP uses a weighting kernel to perform linear approximation [25].

In this research, a Python package named `Captum` [22] is used to implement these model interpretability methods.

3.2   Data Input

The source of data used in the model training process was collected through an experiment led by Liu Yang and her colleagues, which took place from December 15 to 22, 2021, in Nanjing, China. A total of 34 healthy participants aged 14–55 were recruited through social media, and informed consent was obtained from adults and guardians of any teenagers. The experiment adhered to the Declaration of Helsinki guidelines.

Located at Xinjiekou Subway Station in Nanjing's commercial center, the chosen ground space featured four-story commercial buildings on one side and a sidewalk with trees on the other. A preliminary test on December 16, 2021, with four participants validated the experimental design. The remaining 30 participants, 14 males and 16 females, were grouped into six groups and joined the experiment on the days between December 17 to 22.

The participants were briefed on the experiment's purpose and equipped with portable wireless physiological recording devices in order to collect trajectory data upon arrival at the subway station. Subsequently, participants were guided to the station exit and instructed to go to the next road crossing within 10 min. During the walk, participants could freely explore the sidewalk and open spaces but were not allowed to enter buildings. Table 1 shows a sample of the collected trajectory data, and the resultant trajectories are demonstrated in Fig. 1.

Table 1. Data sample of participant trajectories.

Start Time (s)	X (°)	Y (°)
0	118.779357	32.0441735
1	118.779357	32.0441735
2	118.779357	32.0441755
3	118.779356	32.0441778
4	118.779361	32.0441805
5	118.779366	32.0441780

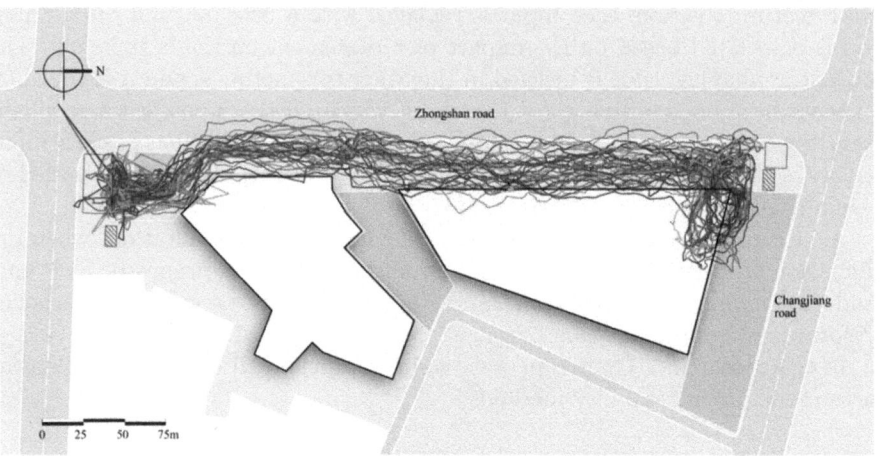

Fig. 1. Trajectories mapped on the site plan.

3.3   Data Preprocessing

One landmark statue on Zhongshan Road is picked as the origin point, with the X axis extending to the north and the Y axis extending to the east. The geodesic distance is then calculated based on the collected trajectory and the proposed reference system so that the positions of the participants are expressed in meters.

Trajectories are then grouped based on their allocation on the day of the experiment. At each time step, the information of N_{slow} and N_{fast} is available to the agent within the same group.

Each trajectory is then divided into adjacent intervals of 5 s by convention [14]. As this research focuses on the distance to green space D_g and the effect of the street wall, any interval that does not include a position within 2 m of green space or a street wall is eliminated. The destination D_d of this interval is set as the position at the last time step.

4   Preliminary Results

The proposed method, which uses model interpretability methods to understand the reward network trained by AIRL, is further tested based on a classical control task, cart pole, in reinforcement learning [4]. The goal of a cart pole is to keep a pole upright as long as possible by moving the cart left and right, which comprise the action space. The state space includes the position and velocity of the cart, and the angle and angular velocity of the pole with respect to the cart.

A trained model provided by [20] is imported into the test. This model has demonstrated successfully keeping the pole upright for the duration of the episode (500 s), and it can be observed from the video that the cart is primarily moving to the right. AIRL is used to retrieve the reward network of this model, and three model interpretability methods are then used to infer the relative attribution of each input feature.

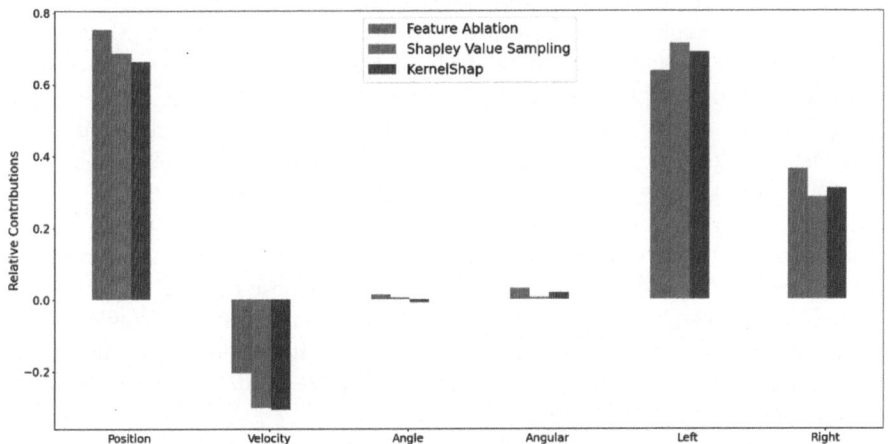

Fig. 2. Relative attributions of reward-network features (CartPole).

The result is presented in Fig. 2. All three methods demonstrate consistency across all the input features besides Angle, where Kernel SHAP shows slight negative contribution while others show slight positive contribution. Velocity has been identified as the major negative contributor to the reward, while Position and Left are the two biggest positive contributors to the reward.

As the cart is primarily moving towards the right, it could be argued that the right action is mainly causing the imbalance of the pole (tilt to the left), and thus, the left action is counteracting to regain balance. This is consistent with the result of the test that the attribution of left action is approximately twice that of the right action.

Consequently, a positive position, indicating the cart is moving to the right, is positively correlated with the reward. However, higher velocity increases imbalance in the pole, resulting in a negative correlation with the reward. Angle and angular velocity have minimal impact on the outcome, as the trained policy effectively maintains stable angles with negligible variation.

5 Discussions and Conclusion

This paper introduces an innovative approach to understand pedestrians' decision-making processes by framing the sum of their reward function along the trajectory as a utility function. Despite the conventional use of IRL for retrieving pedestrians' reward functions, recent progress in training algorithms has shifted towards neural networks. The opaque nature of neural networks necessitates the application of model interpretability techniques to discern the contributions of individual input features. This study advocates a combined method involving AIRL and model interpretability to infer pedestrians' decision-making on urban sidewalks, utilizing trajectory data from prior experiments.

The result of the preliminary test has demonstrated the usage of model interpretability upon explaining the reward network retrieved by AIRL. Similarly, it is reasonable to deduce that an analysis of the pedestrian movement reward net could provide insights into their decision-making process. A figure similar to Fig. 2 can be achieved with the relative contribution from each attribute to the decision making of pedestrian, e.g., the pedestrian values more on the transparency of the street wall over their distance with the green space.

Consequently, the obtained rewards offer valuable insights for urban designers in order to influence pedestrian movements by refining the characteristics of urban streets, with a particular focus on sidewalks. These rewards can be incorporated into pedestrian models, enabling predictions of walking behavior across various urban design scenarios. This integration facilitates decision-making support for designers seeking to enhance the overall pedestrian experience in urban environments.

It is also useful for the obtained reward to be used in multiagent modelling. This result not only enhances traditional social force modelling [18] by providing a reference for the magnitude of the social force, but also serves as a valuable starting point for reward engineering in various scenarios.

In a subsequent step, the construction of pedestrian decision-making on urban sidewalks will be performed, based on the model proposed in 3.1 with the data demonstrated in 3.2. Different scenarios such as subway station or large event gathering will also be examined to explore the proposed method's scalability. Furthermore, as the research at the current stage assumes homogeneity among all the pedestrians, categorizing different types of pedestrians based on the behavior pattern and comparing the focus of their decision-making will also be explored.

Acknowledgments. Liu Yang is funded by the China Postdoctoral Science Foundation (No. 2023M740601), the National Natural Science Foundation of China (No. 52378009), Jiangsu Funding Program for Excellent Postdoctoral Talent (No. 2024ZB363), and the Postdoctoral Fellowship Program of CPSF (GZC20240254).

References

1. Albrecht, S.V., Christianos, F., Schäfer, L.: Multi-Agent Reinforcement Learning: Foundations and Modern Approaches. The MIT Press, Cambridge, Massachusetts (2024)
2. Allievi, W.B.K., Banzhaf, H., Stone, F.S.: Reward (mis)design for autonomous driving. Artif. Intell. **316** (2023)
3. Alsaleh, R., Sayed, T.: Modeling pedestrian-cyclist interactions in shared space using inverse reinforcement learning. Transport. Res. F: Traffic Psychol. Behav. **70**, 37–57 (2020)
4. Barto, A.G., Sutton, R.S., Anderson, C.W.: Neuronlike adaptive elements that can solve difficult learning control problems. Trans. Syst. Man Cybern. **SMC-13**(5), 834–846 (1983)
5. Basu, N., Haque, M.M., King, M., Kamruzzaman, M., Oviedo-Trespalacios, O.: A systematic review of the factors associated with pedestrian route choice. Transp. Rev. **42**(5), 594–672 (2022)
6. Bivina, G.R., Parida, M.: Prioritizing pedestrian needs using a multi-criteria decision approach for a sustainable built environment in the Indian context. Environ. Dev. Sustain. **22**, 4929–4950 (2020)
7. Chalvatzaki, G., Papageorgiou, X.S., Maragos, P., Tzafestas, C.S.: Learn to adapt to human walking: a model-based reinforcement learning approach for a robotic assistant rollator. Robot. Autom. Lett. **4**(4), 3774–3781 (2019)
8. Eschmann, J.: Reward function design in reinforcement learning. In: Belousov, B., Abdulsamad, H., Klink, P., Parisi, S., Peters, J. (eds.) Reinforcement Learning Algorithms: Analysis and Applications, pp. 25–33. Springer (2021)
9. Everett, M., Chen, Y.F., How, J.P.: Collision avoidance in pedestrian-rich environments with deep reinforcement learning. IEEE Access **9**, 10357–10377 (2021)
10. Ewing, R., Hajrasouliha, A., Neckerman, K.M., Purciel-Hill, M., Greene, W.: Streetscape features related to pedestrian activity. J. Plan. Educ. Res. **36**(1), 5–15 (2015)
11. Fahad, M., Chen, Z., Guo, Y.: Learning how pedestrians navigate: a deep inverse reinforcement learning approach. In: Proceedings of a Conference in Madrid (2018)
12. Finn, C., Christiano, P., Abbeel, P., Sutskever, I.: A connection between generative adversarial networks, inverse reinforcement learning, and energy-based models. arXiv preprint https://arxiv.org/abs/1611.03852 (2016)
13. Fu, J., Luo, K., Levine, S.: Learning robust rewards with adversarial inverse reinforcement learning. In: Proceedings of a Conference in Vancouver (2018)
14. Gonon, D., Billard, A.: Inverse reinforcement learning of pedestrian-robot coordination. Robot. Autom. Lett. **8**(8), 4815–4822 (2023)
15. Haghani, M., Sarvi, M.: Pedestrian crowd tactical-level decision making during emergency evacuations. J. Adv. Transp. (2016)
16. Haghani, M., Sarvi, M.: Stated and revealed exit choices of pedestrian crowd evacuees. Transp. Res. Part B: Methodol. **95**, 238–259 (2017)
17. Haghani, M., Sarvi, M.: Imitative (herd) behaviour in direction decision-making hinders efficiency of crowd evacuation processes. Saf. Sci. **114**, 49–60 (2019)
18. Helbing, D., Molnar, P.: Social force model for pedestrian dynamics. Phys. Rev. E **51**(5), 4282–4286 (1995)
19. Ho, J., Ermon, S.: Generative adversarial imitation learning. In: Proceedings of a Conference in Montreal (2016)

20. Hugging Face: PPO Agent playing seals/CartPole-v0. https://huggingface.co/HumanCompatibleAI/ppo-seals-CartPole-v0. Accessed 1 Feb 2024
21. Kim, J., Tak, S., Bierlaire, M., Yeo, H.: Trajectory data analysis on the spatial and temporal influence of pedestrian flow on path planning decision. Sustainability **12**(24) (2020)
22. Kokhlikyan, N., et al.: Captum: a unified and generic model interpretability library for pytorch. arXiv preprint https://arxiv.org/abs/2009.07896 (2020)
23. Liu, Y., Yan, Q., Alahi, A.: Social NCE: contrastive learning of socially-aware motion representations (2021), preprint or unpublished
24. Lovreglio, R., Ronchi, E., Nilsson, D.: A model of the decision-making process during pre-evacuation. Fire Saf. **78**, 168–179 (2015)
25. Lundberg, S.M., Lee, S.I.: A unified approach to interpreting model predictions. In: Advances in Neural Information Processing Systems, vol. 30 (2017)
26. Mohamed, A., Qian, K., Elhoseiny, M., Claudel, C.: Social-STGCNN: a social spatio-temporal graph convolutional neural network for human trajectory prediction (2020), preprint or unpublished
27. Nasernejad, P., Sayed, T., Alsaleh, R.: Modeling pedestrian behavior in pedestrian-vehicle near misses: a continuous gaussian process inverse reinforcement learning (GP-IRL) approach. Accid. Anal. Prev. **161** (2021)
28. Nasernejad, P., Sayed, T., Alsaleh, R.: Multiagent modeling of pedestrian-vehicle conflicts using adversarial inverse reinforcement learning. Transportmetrica A Transp. Sci. **19**(3) (2023)
29. Ng, A.Y., Russell, S.J.: Algorithms for inverse reinforcement learning. In: Proceedings of a Conference in San Francisco (2000)
30. Papadimitriou, E., Lassarre, S., Yannis, G.: Pedestrian risk taking while road crossing: a comparison of observed and declared behaviour. Transp. Res. Procedia **14**, 4354–4363 (2016)
31. Papadimitriou, E., Lassarre, S., Yannis, G.: Human factors of pedestrian walking and crossing behaviour. Transp. Res. Procedia **25**, 2002–2015 (2017)
32. Pérez-D'Arpino, C., Liu, C., Goebel, P., Martín-Martín, R., Savarese, S.: Robot navigation in constrained pedestrian environments using reinforcement learning. In: Proceedings of a Conference in Xi'an (2021)
33. Radha, K., Bansal, M.: Feature fusion and ablation analysis in gender identification of preschool children from spontaneous speech. Circ. Syst. Signal Process. **42**, 6228–6252 (2023)
34. Saleh, K., Hossny, M., Nahavandi, S.: Long-term recurrent predictive model for intent prediction of pedestrians via inverse reinforcement learning. In: Proceedings of a Conference in Canberra (2018)
35. Sheu, Y.h.: Illuminating the black box: Interpreting deep neural network models for psychiatric research. Front. Psychiatry **11** (2020)
36. Soares, F., Silva, E., Pereira, F., Silva, C., Sousa, E., Freitas, E.: To cross or not to cross: impact of visual and auditory cues on pedestrians' crossing decision-making. Transport. Res. F: Traffic Psychol. Behav. **82**, 202–220 (2021)
37. Strumbelj, E., Kononenko, I.: An efficient explanation of individual classifications using game theory. J. Mach. Learn. Res. **11**, 1–18 (2010)
38. Tong, Y., Bode, N.W.F.: The principles of pedestrian route choice. J. R. Soc. Interface **19**(189) (2022)
39. Wedagamaa, D.M.P., Bennettb, S., Dissanayake, D.: Analyzing pedestrian perceptions towards traffic safety using discrete choice models. Int. J. Adv. Sci. Eng. Inf. Technol. **10**(6) (2020)

40. Yang, Y., Sun, J.: Study on pedestrian red-time crossing behavior: integrated field observation and questionnaire data. Transp. Res. Record J. Transp. Res. Board **2393**(1) (2013)
41. Zhangl, G., Yu, Z., Jin, D., Li, Y.: Physics-infused machine learning for crowd simulation. In: Proceedings of the 28th ACM SIGKDD Conference on Knowledge Discovery and Data Mining (2022)

Author Index

J. Thompson and I. Stankov (Eds.): MABS 2024, LNAI 15583, p. 99, 2025.
https://doi.org/10.1007/978-3-031-88017-9